PRIVACY IN A FREE SOCIETY

FINAL REPORT

ANNUAL CHIEF JUSTICE EARL WARREN CONFERENCE
ON ADVOCACY IN THE UNITED STATES

JUNE 7-8, 1974

Sponsored by

THE ROSCOE POUND-AMERICAN TRIAL LAWYERS FOUNDATION
20 Garden Street, Cambridge, Massachusetts 02138

ry of Congress Catalog Card Number: 74-19797

Printing of this Report made possible through the financial assistance of IBM - International Business Machines Corporation and ATLA - The Association of Trial Lawyers of America.

CONTENTS

Foreword

It is time for America to "look homeward." The cannonade of revelations these past two years warns us that we have not begun to understand the implications of democracy. For the sake of the future, we must be held accountable. We must respond.

What has come to be known as the Watergate Affair brought to a climax an era that started at the end of World War II and was directed toward the objective of materialistic values.

Both technology with its surging, seemingly uncontrollable momentum and the arrogance of ambitious politicians threatened the viability of individual rights — among them the right to privacy.

But the fault does not lie entirely with the men of technology, or with the self-serving politicians — it lies with us all. We have not sought the power of reason. It may be that we are in a "crisis of reason." We turned away from the principles of a moral democracy that places the dignity of its citizenry above all else. Thus, today more than ever, we must reflect upon and examine every activity of American life to learn its decisive influence on an open society.

It was in this spirit that the Annual Chief Justice Earl Warren Conference on Advocacy this year undertook to dialog on the subject: PRIVACY IN A FREE SOCIETY.

The Conference was held at the Roscoe Pound-American Trial Lawyers Research Center in Cambridge on June 7 and June 8. Discussions were focused on three areas — Data Banks and Dossiers, Electronic Surveillance, and Political Informing and other kinds of Spying. Each part was examined primarily for its effect and infringement on individual privacy.

In preparation for the Conference we sought three of our country's authorities on the subject to prepare background papers that would serve as take-off points for discussion. We thank them for giving so generously of their time and knowledge.

They are: Professor Arthur R. Miller, Professor of Law, Harvard University who wrote on "The Right of Privacy: Data Banks and Dossiers"; Professor Herman Schwartz, Professor of Law, State University of New York at Buffalo on "Reflections on Six Years of Legitimated Electronic Surveillance"; Frank J. Donner, Director of the American Civil Liberties Union Project on Political Surveillance, Yale Law School on "Political Intelligence: Cameras, Informers and Files."

These papers were distributed to 51 invited Conferees prior to the Conference. Thus, when they met, they commenced to review the theses stated and went on to explore new directions and come forth with various conclusions. The Conferees were not held to the principles set forth by the papers. (The background papers follow the Final Recommendations of the Conference in this publication.)

When we discuss "the right to privacy" here in America, perhaps more so than anywhere else, there are many interlocking problems. We recognize that technological application is certainly not all evil — it has brought mankind great wonders.

Because of the complexities, the Conference sought interdisciplinary critical examination of the subject. To this end, the Conference brought together people of various associated fields with diverse experiences. They included: computer scientists, law enforcement officials, law professors, lawyers (government, public interest and private sectors), industry spokesmen, U.S. congressmen, journalists, political scientists, judges and philosophers.

The Conference followed its prescribed format: the Conferees were divided into three groups in order to encourage active participation by each person. Each group discussed the three topics separately, with the writer of each background paper. Following the group meetings, all were invited to meet in a plenary session. The conclusions of each individual group were discussed and the Final Recommendations of the entire Conference were concluded.

Every Conference needs talented people to keep it within its format and accomplish the maximum within a limited time. For doing this so well, we are grateful to the people who served as group chairmen: Dr. Edward J. Bloustein, president, Rutgers University; Dr. Norman Fredericksen, director, Psychological Studies Division, Educational Testing Service; Professor H. Richard Uviller, Columbia University School of Law.

To the rapporteurs, those who had the difficult task of recording and summarizing the Findings and Recommendations, we extend our deep appreciation. These are: Nat Hentoff, journalist; Professor L. Thorne McCarty, Assistant Professor, Faculty of Law and Jurisprudence, State University of New York at Buffalo; and Professor Gary T. Marx, Associate Professor, Department of Urban Studies and Planning (sociology), Massachusetts Institute of Technology.

After the two-day meeting, a draft of the Recommendations formulated at the plenary session was circulated by mail to all Conferees. The majority of the Conferees returned the draft indicating their acceptance, some returned it making a note of dissent regarding certain recommendations; others expressed their dissent with comments. We have included some dissents with comments and additional explanations in footnotes.

History has taught us that dissent and disagreements must be aired whether they come from the lay citizenry or the Supreme Court. It is Justice Brandeis' dissent written in 1928 that we still turn to today to better understand the "right to privacy."

> **A consensus was reached on the three parts of the Conference.**
> **The Recommendations are not to be construed as the exact views**
> **of each Conferee.**

Included in this Report are Recommendations that were adopted overwhelmingly by the Conferees along with those that were adopted narrowly. It is understandable that the knowledgeable people who gathered at our Center here in

Cambridge, speaking from different experiences, would have differences of opinion. Nevertheless a consensus was reached.

As a Foundation, we do not advocate a particular stand. However, we recognize our responsibility and the trust placed in us as stewards of this Foundation to make the opportunity possible for research — to bring forth the ideas and thoughts of cultivated minds — to bring together people who will sit and reason and place the dignity of man uppermost in our country's list of concerns.

The Foundation will distribute this Report throughout the country to our educational institutions, governmental agencies, lay organizations, news media and others. In so doing, we hope that those who can effectuate change will consider the Findings and Recommendations set forth.

In the hope of furthering the understanding of some of the unprecedented problems our nation is encountering today in the area of electronic surveillance, we chose to publish the comments of William C. Sullivan, former Assistant to the Director of the Federal Bureau of Investigation (No. 3 man). Mr. Sullivan served with the FBI for thirty years. Illness prevented him from attending the Conference. His comments and recommendations are his own and are presented herein as entirely separate from the Findings and Recommendations of the Conference.

It is with deep appreciation that we acknowledge the men and women who joined in this Conference. They prove that America does have the intellectual faculties and the desire to preserve the right to privacy.

Herbert H. Bennett
President, The Roscoe Pound-American
Trial Lawyers Foundation

Theodore I. Koskoff
Chairman, Annual Chief Justice
Earl Warren Conference 1974

FINAL REPORT
PRIVACY IN A FREE SOCIETY

PART A

RECOMMENDATIONS
ELECTRONIC SURVEILLANCE

Summary

(Note: Final Recommendations on Electronic Surveillance emanating from the Conference together with commentaries follow this summary.)

The Conference undertook the study of electronic surveillance in two areas — domestic intelligence and law enforcement. The Conference expressed strong opposition to electronic surveillance for domestic intelligence purposes. It opposed, by a narrow margin, the use of electronic surveillance for law enforcement purposes.

In discussing two methods of electronic surveillance, the Conferees were opposed to both telephone tapping and room bugging. However, they felt that room bugging was more insidious than telephone tapping because of the much greater and less controllable invasion of privacy resulting from room surveillance.

A broad consensus of the Conferees revealed general skepticism toward electronic surveillance as a tool and towards methods for control of its use. It is interesting to note that this general skepticism was shown among members of such a diverse group including many with long experience in law enforcement and in law. The opponents of electronic surveillance based their conclusions on a belief that electronic surveillance was of relatively little value to conventional law enforcement, was used primarily for minor offenses, produced very serious invasions of privacy, and was quite difficult to control. It should be noted that there was some discussion about the validity of the available statistics, which indicated that electronic surveillance was invoked most often in cases of "minor offenses."

There were Conferees supporting some electronic surveillance for law enforcement purposes, who believed that the technique should be used only for crimes of the utmost gravity and only if controls are strengthened and, together with those currently in the statute, are more effectively enforced.

The Conference stressed that, if there were to be any electronic surveillance, regardless of its form, of American citizens, it should be only with prior judicial scrutiny and approval — with a court order. A substantial majority recommended that no surveillance for intelligence purposes be permitted. However, if any electronic surveillance were authorized, it should be only for solving specific crimes and not for obtaining general intelligence about particular individuals or groups.

The Conference also overwhelmingly recommended a series of procedural and other controls. It suggested a requirement that, whatever federal electronic surveillance is done, it should be conducted only by the Department of Justice, subject to criteria and procedures examined at public hearings, and under close scrutiny by congressional committees. Also, the Conference urged that persons subjected to illegal electronic surveillance be permitted to recover damages from the governmental agencies engaging in such activity.

RECOMMENDATION I

There should be no electronic surveillance for domestic intelligence purposes.[1]

(Adopted by substantial majority)

Commentary: While disagreement remained as to whether electronic surveillance, with restrictions, is permissible when related to detection and prosecution of specific crimes, a majority of the Conferees determined that electronic surveillance for domestic intelligence should not be permissible.

---

1. Mr. Michael Kenney wanted to be on record as being opposed to all electronic surveillance. His single Recommendation in this area would be: "There should be *no* electronic surveillance."

RECOMMENDATION II

There should be no electronic surveillance for law enforcement purposes.[1]

(Adopted by narrow margin)

Commentary: This vote represents the fundamental division among the Conferees. While there was general skepticism regarding the effectiveness of electronic surveillance, a narrow majority believed that law enforcement authorities should not be allowed to use electronic surveillance even for crime detection purposes, and a minority believed that electronic surveillance should remain available for law enforcement, though this group insisted that it be used only for very serious offenses, and under very strict controls. There was a group of Conferees who, whatever their individual predilections on this issue, made the point that our current knowledge concerning electronic surveillance at all levels of law enforcement (federal, state and local) is inadequate. Additional empirical studies are needed to determine the extent and the effectiveness of its use.

---

1. Mr. Kenneth Conboy dissents from this Recommendation and adds the following statement: "I cannot subscribe to the dubious logic of the proposition that, because too many gambling warrants have been issued in the past several years, no authority, regardless of how circumscribed in execution, should be vested in the courts to issue warrants in cases involving, for example, imminent bombings, aircraft hijacks, random killings or barbarous political murders."

Ms. Mary C. Lawton wished it noted that she abstains on propositions relating to electronic surveillance. She felt that more precise definitions of terms used in the discussions were needed.

RECOMMENDATION III

State and local authorities should not be allowed to engage in electronic surveillance.[1]

(Vote evenly divided)

Commentary: There was a sharp split over whether state and local law enforcement officials (as opposed to federal officials) really need electronic surveillance, whether they have used it excessively and indiscriminately, and whether the judicial and other controls in the statute do or can function properly on the state level.

---

1. Mr. Conboy did not support the Recommendation because "the data supports the conclusion that state authorities have been more discriminating in the use of electronic surveillance than federal authorities. For example, the huge number of gambling warrants obtained were predominantly obtained by the FBI. Also, jurisdiction for the most serious crime in terms of penalty – murder – is almost exclusively with state officials."

RECOMMENDATION IV

No electronic surveillance should be carried out without a court order for any purpose on American citizens on United States soil or on American citizens in foreign countries.

(Adopted overwhelmingly)

Commentary: The Conferees drew attention here to the Supreme Court's decision in *United States vs. U.S. District Court*, 407 U.S. 297, 92 S. Ct. 2125, 32 L. Ed. 2d 752 (1972), which suggested in an 8-0 decision that, in all cases of electronic surveillance on American citizens or organizations for intelligence purposes, that is, for purposes unrelated to solution of a specific crime, a court order is required. Also, the Executive Branch has no inherent power to invade a citizen's right to privacy without satisfying an impartial magistrate that a justification exists for such an intrusion.

This Recommendation expresses the Conference's conviction that there be *no* warrantless electronic surveillance, under any circumstances on American citizens.

RECOMMENDATION V

To the extent that electronic surveillance is permitted for law enforcement purposes, it should be limited to crimes of the utmost gravity.

(Adopted by large majority)

Commentary: While there was some discussion on the meaning of "crimes of utmost gravity," the Conference reached no final definition of the concept, except that it would almost certainly include an imminent threat to life.

RECOMMENDATION VI

If used at all, electronic surveillance for law enforcement purposes should be permitted only by court order and on probable cause subject to the following conditions:

A) It must be directly related to specific criminal acts or activities;

B) There must be a specific limitation of the time during which the device remains in place or in use; and the length of time permitted should be the shortest possible;

C) There must be a definite demonstration of the need for installation of the device;

D) There must be no other law enforcement technique available for obtaining the information, and the applicant must demonstrate this fully;

E) There must be restraint — responsible action and accurate reporting by the law enforcement officials carrying out the order.

(Adopted overwhelmingly)

Commentary: This Recommendation reflects specific problems in the present operation of the electronic surveillance statute, and is intended to supplement and make more effective the statutory controls.

RECOMMENDATION VII

Even when electronic surveillance is used with regard to crimes of utmost gravity, there should be no electronic surveillance of rooms — no bugging of a room.

(Adopted by large majority)

Commentary: Bugging should *not* be utilized under any circumstances. Bugging was seen as a more serious invasion of privacy than wiretapping since, while one can refrain from using a telephone and thereby avoid a wiretap, the presence of a room bug in one's home or office makes it impossible to be free from surveillance.[1]

---

1. Mr. Conboy dissented from this Recommendation and explained how he saw its result: "the law would simultaneously authorize (wiretapping) and condemn (room bugging) electronic surveillance of the imminent criminal, contingent solely upon the mode (phone conversation or face to face meeting) selected by him."

RECOMMENDATION VIII

If any federal electronic surveillance is to be permitted, the authority for all warrants for wiretapping should be limited to a single governmental agency — the United States Justice Department. The Justice Department should be the only federal agency to install wiretaps on United States soil and on American citizens abroad.[1]

(Adopted overwhelmingly)

Commentary: Since electronic surveillance is difficult to detect in the first place, a proliferation of federal agencies engaged in wiretapping would ineluctably result in more privacy abuses than would result if all legal wiretapping were the responsibility of only one agency.

The Conferees were mindful of the diversity of government agencies engaged in electronic surveillance which were uncovered during the Watergate investigations — some of them accountable to no one but the President — with the Justice Department and the courts being entirely bypassed.

---

1. Professor John Elliff suggests that "the United States Department of Justice should not be the agency to install wiretaps overseas, since its investigative jurisdiction is primarily within the United States. However, the Attorney General might properly be required to approve any wiretaps installed by another agency on American citizens abroad."

RECOMMENDATION IX

The procedures and criteria by which wiretaps and other forms of eavesdropping are sought, and warrants for their use issued, should be clearly and properly prescribed by the United States Justice Department only after complete public hearings on these procedures and criteria, such hearings to be held in various parts of the country.

(Adopted overwhelmingly)

Commentary: If the Justice Department is established as the only agency with the responsibility for federal electronic surveillance, the citizenry should be made aware of this. Furthermore, the citizenry should be made aware of the precise processes by which eavesdropping is permitted by the courts and carried out by the Justice Department. In this way the widespread fear that government eavesdropping is pervasive can be countered by a precise vesting of limited authority — and accountability for any abuse of that authority — in this one agency.

RECOMMENDATION X

A very strong congressional oversight committee should be established in both branches of Congress to review all wiretaps by federal agencies. This would apply to the United States Justice Department if it were established that it were the only governmental agency authorized to wiretap.

(Adopted unanimously)

Commentary: The unanimous approval of this Recommendation reflects the strong conviction of the Conferees concerning the establishment of an active monitoring system by Congress — representatives selected by the citizenry — to ensure accountability on the part of those involved in limited, carefully restricted, use of electronic surveillance.[1]

_____

1. Mr. William D. Ruckelshaus informed the Conference, that "not once, in the eighty days during which I was Acting Director of the FBI, was I called on to testify before Congress about the FBI's involvement in electronic surveillance. It is not in the public interest for any such activity to go unmonitored by the Congress."

RECOMMENDATION XI

A reporting system should be undertaken by the Justice Department, subject to proper regulations to maintain confidentiality, so that all information disclosed by taps can be given to Congress for it to properly exercise its oversight function.

(Adopted unanimously)

Commentary: The information would include: the duration of the wiretap; the need for the tap; an affidavit submitted for the issuance of a warrant for the tap; the authorization by the Attorney General of specific taps; what information the tap revealed and the consequences of the tap, that is, whether there was an arrest, conviction or any other disposition.

RECOMMENDATION XII

A specific minimum amount of damages, plus attorney's fees, should be available for any violation of the wiretapping or other eavesdropping statutes by federal, state or local officials. These damages should be recoverable in a federal court from the particular governmental agency engaged in such eavesdropping.

(Adopted overwhelmingly)

Commentary: The Conferees believed that effective sanctions must be provided against all who violate statutes concerning the use of electronic surveillance.

PART B

RECOMMENDATIONS
POLITICAL INFORMING

Note: The Conference discussions underscored the great complexity of the issues around political informing. During the general discussion the point was made that there is a **difference between informing undertaken for political reasons or motives and informing conducted on political activities.** The Conferees felt that informing for political reasons should not be condoned under any circumstances. Therefore, the Recommendations which follow deal with **informing on political activities.**

After serious deliberation, the Conferees almost unanimously agreed on two strong Recommendations. Also, a proposal, which had substantial support but fell just short of passing, is included for future serious study. A commentary follows.

RECOMMENDATION XIII

Every government agency should be barred from collecting any data concerning political activity, association, or expression — protected under the First Amendment — and should destroy any such data now in existence in both legislative and executive agencies.[1]

(Adopted overwhelmingly)

---

1. Dr. Margaret Lantis would clarify the phrase "collecting any data" to mean "any data not of public record."

RECOMMENDATION XIV

There should be no use and placement of a human agent for surreptitious surveillance, except upon court order based on probable cause and subject to the same restraints and restrictions as the use and employment of surreptitious electronic eavesdropping devices and techniques now provided for by the Omnibus Crime Bill [1]

(Adopted overwhelmingly)

---

1. Two Conferees felt strongly about this Recommendation. Mr. Michael Kenney in this regard said, "Lots of indications that Omnibus Crime Bill is pretty frail reed."

Also Professor John Elliff contends that "this Recommendation fails adequately to distinguish among various forms of 'human surveillance' such as the occasional source of information, the periodic informant, the regular informer, and the planted undercover agent. A judicial warrant procedure is workable only for the deliberately planted undercover agent, as in the circumstances of *Hoffa v. United States*, 385 U.S. 293 (1966). To attempt to require a warrant procedure in less clearly defined cases would unduly hamper the flexibility needed for effective law enforcement."

Although defeated, the following proposal is included to indicate the direction of the discussion and to provoke further study.

An independent executive agency should be established with authority to insure compliance with Recommendation XIII and to supervise activities in accordance with Recommendation XIV; it should have a mechanism to receive and act upon complaints from citizens.[1]

(Very narrowly defeated)

---

1. Dr. Edward Bloustein commented: "I oppose this proposal on the grounds it provides for a proliferation of enforcement agencies without any basis for believing the evil in this instance is greater than others where a comparable form of oversight might be required."

Commentary: The Conferees were concerned not only with the planting of informants in political groups but also with such techniques as photography of peaceful demonstrators and maintenance of political intelligence databanks. The uncontrolled use of these techniques by police was seen as a severe threat to First Amendment freedoms.

The Conferees stressed that a citizen's First Amendment rights are seriously undermined when authorities have unrestricted license to engage in the surveillance of lawful political activities. This interference with First Amendment rights has often been the result of political intelligence activities of the Federal Bureau of Investigation (FBI) and many local police departments. Some Conferees asserted that political intelligence activities have become largely an end in themselves, divorced from judicial cases or policy needs, and serve primarily to stifle dissent. In addition, they necessarily divert law enforcement resources which might better be used elsewhere.

Such surveillance inspires fear and distrust, inhibits political involvement of moderates and the uncommitted, and can stimulate a self-censorship not in keeping with a free society.

The Conference considered in different group meetings various factors which were cited as having helped produce an aura of fear and distrust in our society. Some of these are:

- the expanded role of the professional policeman which stresses the need for the autonomy of police agents

- the abdication of executive, legislative, and judicial oversight

- the increased potential, both technologically (e.g., with sophisticated cameras, eavesdropping equipment and the like), and organizationally (e.g., through regional and national police data sharing, improved communications, and vastly increased police budgets) to engage in surveillance

- a lack of understanding of the Bill of Rights by public officials, the police, and a significant segment of the public

- exaggeration of the threat posed by protest groups and the tendency to equate dissent with subversion. This includes a "be prepared" cold war vision of the world which sees conspiracy everywhere and believes that an apocalyptic day of reckoning will soon come between the forces of good and evil. Authorities feel that they must be on their guard and "get them, before they get us."

With respect to political data currently held, the Conferees generally agreed that this information is often inaccurate, outdated, and incomplete. It may be based on biased sources and is not collected by neutral observers. Few checks on its validity exist, and controls over access to it are far from perfect.

During the discussions it was pointed out that procedures for gathering such data, and the volume of data gathered, often intensify during periods of social conflict. Rather than receding as conflict subsides, both the techniques and the data collected become institutionalized and take on a life of their own. Vested interests develop that perpetuate political intelligence activities, even as the threat diminishes. This tendency, the Conferees felt, must be checked.

The Conferees recognized that objections to the banning of political surveillance may be raised; it may be feared that in periods of intense domestic and international conflict, limitations on the political intelligence activities of police and other agencies may mean increased disorder and threats to the stability of the state. But they noted that historically this has not proven to be the case. During the 1924-1939 period of domestic conflict, the FBI was prohibited from gathering domestic intelligence information without dire consequences to America's freedom.

The Conferees accepted the premise that in a democracy, a degree of risk is unavoidable. Indeed, the hallmark of a police state is its effort to totally eliminate all risks to the state.[1] There are clearly trade-offs here.

The task of authorities is, of course, difficult. The violent rhetoric and grandiose claims of a small proportion of protestors (some of them police agents) may feed and also provide some apparent justification for official paranoia and the belief, held by some authorities, in the existence of a world-wide conspiracy. In this regard, the Conferees examined the question of what type of law enforcement attention, if any, should be directed toward a group that consistently makes violent threats, and states its intention to engage in criminal activity.

---

1. Professor Harry Howe Ransom points out that "a viable democracy must be willing to take enormous risks with political dissent and even potential subversion. Violent behavior is and should be illegal and controlled. But if we maintain that a policy of deterrence for potential political subversion is necessary, we have taken a long step toward a totalitarian state. There is perhaps a greater danger to political liberties from 'Middle America' acting out of fear of radical ideas or possible revolutionary action than from the real or imagined behavior or intentions of real radicals or revolutionaries. But the main point is that we must be willing to take substantial risks with political dissent if we are to preserve the Bill of Rights. A police strategy of political deterrence is unacceptable in America."

The Conferees accepted the fact that attention such as some contact between the authorities and those planning a demonstration is often required – to determine the route to be followed, to insure the flow of traffic, to provide for emergency medical care and sanitary facilities, and to protect demonstrators from those who would attack them. Knowledge of the probable size of a crowd, duration of a demonstration, its purpose, and leaders may be needed to protect protest. Where a disruption by counter demonstrators is anticipated, it may become necessary to use cameras to photograph them and, in so doing, peaceful marchers will be included. The inhibiting effect of surveillance on legitimate political behavior must be weighed against the increased likelihood of arresting those responsible for real violations of law.

The Conferees agreed that police cannot be expected to ignore public protest events any more than they would ignore a large parade. They have a legitimate right to gather very limited information,[1] which should be kept only for a short period of time. It should be restricted to information needed for short-run peacekeeping purposes and this type of limited "intelligence" gathering is very different from the kinds the Conference recommended be abolished. Yet, a visible police presence at a demonstration and the police gathering prior information about it, may still have chilling effects. It is important to educate both demonstrators and police as to the justified reasons for police presence and to develop mechanisms to insure that police, in seeking to protect civil liberties, do not end up destroying them.

The Conference concluded that authorities must be better educated in the freedoms of the Bill of Rights and the need for judicial, legislative, and executive control over their actions. Also, citizens may not know of their rights. Schools must do much more in teaching children about their rights to freedom of association, speech, and due process.

Relating specifically to Recommendation XIV the Conference concluded that, just as a judge now must issue a warrant based on probable cause before electronic eavesdropping can be carried out, police should have to obtain a similar warrant before planting an informer in a group. A major factor concerning informer abuse is that now their use is subjected to nothing more than the whims of the police agency. The purpose of this Recommendation is to control police use of informers through judicial means. Some Conferees questioned whether it should be left to the courts to decide when such techniques should be used.

---

1. Ms. Catherine G. Roraback disagreed that the police function should include the gathering of any information. Rather, she said their legitimate purpose is "regulating traffic and keeping the peace."

Authorities may resort to subterfuge to gain the desired warrant by basing the information they give to the judge on reports of non-existent informants. Warrants may be obtained on loosely-worded criminal statutes such as conspiracy to encourage others to cross state lines to riot. Police may be able to shop around for a judge who would readily grant a warrant, and local judges may not be sufficiently detached. However, a warrant at least provides a record of the extent of surveillance, even if later a judge overturns it. Some Conferees felt that requiring executive approval through the Attorney General (at the federal level) would be a more visible and preferable means of control. A very small minority of the Conferees felt that the police should exercise control over themselves through internal administrative mechanisms with legislative oversight.

Because of its vast scope and the massive amount of data already on file, many of the Conferees felt a need for an independent agency to monitor surveillance activities. In considering a monitoring agency in the area of political surveillance, the Conferees examined the following concepts:

- Should a monitoring agency be a part of government or a semi-autonomous commission? Also, should the agency be in the executive or legislative branch of government?

Although self-regulation appeared an ideal solution, the majority of the Conferees agreed that it is unrealistic to expect government agencies to voluntarily give up a practice which is conducted in secret and which they see as a necessary means of obtaining what they view as their goals.

- Would an agency even be necessary, were there to be judicial control over police use of informers?

A minority of the Conferees felt that judicial control over police use of informers, were it to be established, would be adequate.

Many of those present, while favoring the idea of a regulatory body in principle felt that the Conference did not have the time and information needed to make useful recommendations as to the specific form of such a body.

The Conferees did discuss the various types of agencies that could best monitor this activity, and whether there was a need for statutorily-prescribed remedies for redress in the case of unauthorized surveillance. Although no definite conclusion was reached about the establishment of an independent agency, or the specific nature of such an agency, there was considerable support among the Conferees for such action.

PART C

RECOMMENDATIONS
DATA BANKS AND DOSSIERS

Summary

(Note: Specific Recommendations along with commentaries follow this summary.)

The Conferees agreed, first of all, on the nature of the threat posed by an efficient information technology in contemporary American society. Although never put to a vote, a common diagnosis of the problems of informational privacy emerged from the group discussions.[1] The Conferees referred frequently to critical decisions about individuals which were now being made on the basis of inaccurate, incomplete or irrelevant information. They expressed their concern that information systems would become much more highly integrated and centralized in the years to come, thus magnifying the potential dangers. And, they suggested that an increased quantity of stored personal data, even if complete and accurate, would lead to a substantial increase of power among data-collecting agencies, and would create among the citizenry a "dossier mentality" — people making decisions and fashioning their behavior in order to enhance their record image for data collectors. These propositions, and others like them, were not explicitly debated by the Conferees, but were used as a starting point for a thorough discussion of the possible remedies. The critical debate thus focused on the search for solutions to these problems of informational privacy.

---

1. Ms. Dorothy Glancy defined "informational privacy" as "the control individuals exercise over the collection and use of personal information about themselves."

There was also agreement on the question of remedies, at least at a general level. The Conferees agreed onRecommendations including several principles of fair information practice, the necessity of federal legislation embodying these principles and regulating almost all information handlers, and the need to enforce this legislation both by a private cause of action and by a governmental administrative agency, which can be an existing agency.

As the discussion groups debated the application of the Recommendations to specific fact situations, a number of difficulties emerged. How does one determine what information is relevant for a particular purpose? How does one handle conflicts of privacy, i.e. conflicts between those who maintain records and believe they should be strictly private and subjects who believe they should have access to their records? What specific powers should a federal agency be given?

It became clear that it would be difficult to reach a consensus on some of these questions — not so much because of irreconcilable differences of opinion, but because the solutions would require drawing lines and drafting standards of considerable complexity, a task demanding more time than the two-day Conference allowed.

Nevertheless, what is striking about these discussions is the overwhelming support given to the following powerful Recommendations and approaches, and the clear conviction that the more complex details could be worked out eventually, given time, patience, and good will.

RECOMMENDATION XV

Every organization, whether public or private, which processes personal information — information which can be directly referenced to an individual — whether automated or manual, should be bound by the following principles:

A

The data collector should owe every data subject a legally recognized fiduciary duty of reasonable care and fair dealing.

(Adopted by nearly unanimous vote)

B

The data collector should collect only that information which is demonstrably necessary and relevant to a proper purpose of the organization.

(Adopted by nearly unanimous vote)

C

The data collector should provide adequate systems for data security, including technical, administrative, and personnel safeguards.

(Adopted by nearly unanimous vote)

D

The data collector should provide every data subject with a right of access to his own file, plus procedures for challenging and correcting erroneous or irrelevant information. [1]

(Adopted by nearly unanimous vote)

E

The data collector should destroy or seal all obsolete information. [2]

(Adopted by nearly unanimous vote)

Commentary: It was understood by the Conferees that the principles would require detailed elaboration, and possibly a few exceptions in particular stiuations. Nevertheless, the overwhelming vote for the principles of Recommendation **XV** indicates strong support for the basic policies embodied herein, and carries with it the implication that exceptions should be granted only for very compelling reasons. The principles of Recommendation **XV** were not intended by the Conferees as absolute rules capable of mechanical application.

---

1. Dr. Edward J. Bloustein commented: "I disagree insofar as the file contains material solicited from others on a confidential basis."

2. Mr. Vance Packard expressed the following opinion: "To a bureaucrat no information ever becomes obsolete. There is no telling when it could be useful." Therefore, he suggests "requiring a review of all data stored every five years and requiring that all data be discarded unless there is a clear justification for holding it."

A few Conferees were concerned about the data subject's right of access in Recommendation XV-D (The data collector should provide every data subject with a right of access to his own file, plus procedures for challenging and correcting erroneous or irrelevant information.[1]) It was pointed out that such a provision could lead to conflicts of privacy in many cases. For example, a number of Conferees felt that teachers and employers required some assurance of confidentiality in writing letters of reference. If these letters became generally available to the data subjects, one would expect them to become uniformly bland, while the important information would be communicated orally. Similarly, medical records have traditionally been kept secret from patients, largely because of a concern that a doctor's uninterpreted diagnostic notes would interfere with the treatment of many diseases. Several Conferees reported that in Massachusetts, where patients have recently gained access to their records, doctors have begun keeping separate files, one for disclosure and one for their more sensitive medical data.

Several possible approaches to these conflicts of privacy were suggested. The confidentiality of letters of reference might be protected simply by exempting small, personal files from the access principle. The Conferees did not want to see an enforceable legal rule applying to everyone's personal filing cabinet. The accuracy of medical records could be insured by a third-party inspection, performed by a physician of the patient's choice, at least where there would be possible medical harm resulting from direct access. In another area of concern, however, agreement seemed harder to come by. Many Conferees would exempt "active criminal investigatory files" — which include criminal justice intelligence and analytical files — from the data subject's access. Those who held this position leaned toward such an exemption because of the belief that such information systems do have a proper place in our society — when properly utilized — but are unique in their operation and function. Consequently, they must be treated separately.

---

1. Mr. Michael Kenney pointed out that those who would not support a data subject's right of access to his own file may be concerned only with their own activities. He believes "personal exemptions quickly lead to no rights at all."

Several Conferees also expressed reservations about the determination of "relevance"which would be required by Recommendation XV-B (The data collector should collect only that information which is demonstrably necessary and relevant to a proper purpose of the organization.), and, to some extent, by Recommendation XV-E (The data collector should destroy or seal all obsolete information.) It is clear that the relevance of a piece of information for a certain purpose depends on numerous factors, and varies widely among the numerous areas to which these principles would apply (credit, insurance, employment, education, welfare, criminal, medical, etc.). It is unlikely that the simple word "relevance" would provide sufficient guidelines, either to the parties or to the courts; it is unlikely that much more precise statutory standards could be developed to cover all the contemplated areas of application; but it is possible that an administrative agency could develop sufficient expertise in the most important of these areas to draft appropriate regulations in each one.[1] And yet, a number of Conferees were reluctant to grant a federal agency the power to intrude to this extent on the decision-making processes of all public and private institutions. One discussion group debated this problem at length, with no resolution.

---

1. In this regard Dr. Robert M. Fano stated: "The determination of what information is necessary and relevant presents difficult problems, indeed, because it requires balancing the benefits resulting from the information in question with the damage to privacy done by its collection. When Government is involved, this balancing is a political decision that should be made in the legislation authorizing the activities for which the information is to be collected and used. Most often there are several ways of achieving the same general objective which, however, may differ significantly in the amount and sensitivity of the personal information required. Welfare legislation is a good example. In the private sector, consumer protection agencies could deal with the fairness of requests for information from the public as they do now with the safety of products and the validity of the claims made about them. I doubt very much that general rules can be invented for determining the necessity and relevancy of information, or that a single Government agency can be entrusted with the promulgation of specific rules across the board."

RECOMMENDATION XVI

There should be enacted a federal code of fair information practices, which would closely regulate the collection, storage, dissemination and use of personal information, and which thereby would protect the individual's right to privacy, confidentiality and due process.

(Adopted by nearly unanimous vote)

Commentary: Given a commitment to the principles set forth in Recommendation **XV** there are several possible means of implementation (1) further development of common law and constitutional doctrine; (2) increased self-regulation; and (3) enactment of state and federal legislation. It was generally believed that common law and constitutional development are inadequate to the task. The common law of privacy has concerned itself primarily with the very different problems of the mass media, and the development of a thorough and adequate constitutional concept of informational privacy seems unlikely now in light of the Supreme Court's decision in *California Bankers Association vs. Schultz*, ___ U.S. ___ , 94 S. Ct. 1494, 39 L. Ed. 2d 812, (1974).

   A number of Conferees stressed the importance of education and self-regulation, and pointed to evidence of increased concern among professional data collectors about the implications of their work. It was clear that the Conference as a whole supported these efforts. The Conferees agreed almost unanimously that the only adequate way to achieve a balance between data collection and individual rights was by the enactment of legislation, preferably at the federal level.

It was understood that the proposed legislation would incorporate the five basic principles of Recommendation **XV** and would expand these principles to handle the problems previously discussed. One piece of legislation referred to frequently as a model was H.R. 14163, the comprehensive Right to Privacy Act introduced by Congressmen Barry M. Goldwater, Jr., and Edward I. Koch in April, 1974 and since then modified and re-introduced. The provisions of the original bill (H.R. 14163) served as reference points in the consideration of specific legislative problems.[1]

RECOMMENDATION XVII

Collection of data by single individuals for essentially personal purposes should be exempt from any legislation.

(Adopted by unanimous vote)

Commentary: The Conferees did not want any law, rule, or regulation to cover personal files maintained for personal, private use. The exception for small personal files is intended to alleviate some of the problems of conflicts of privacy. Other possible exceptions were discussed in the individual groups, but never put to a vote before the entire body.

---

1. Professor Harry Howe Ransom set forth the dilemma presented by the accelerating rise of data banks and dossiers, stating: "One horn of the dilemma comes from the fact that most of us want convenience of instant credit or airline/hotel reservations. The price we pay for this convenience in privacy terms may ultimately be higher than we imagine or wish to pay. The other horn is that controlling this danger by creating Federal statutes and administrative rule-making agencies may invite a 'Big Brother' to enter our homes and offices to control abuses. But Big Brother, exercising these controls, could turn out to be worse, in terms of costs to individual freedom and confidentiality of papers, than those abuses that we seek to control. Let us try to be sure that the side effects of controls or 'cures' are not more destructive to liberty than the ills caused by a data bank and dossier society."

RECOMMENDATION XVIII

For violations of the statutory standards of fair information practices, there should be available to data subjects a private right of legal action, with provision for counsel fees,[1] and with federal jurisdiction without regard to the amount in controversy.

(Adopted by nearly unanimous vote)

In addition, the code of fair information practices should be implemented and enforced by a federal agency.

(Adopted by nearly unanimous vote)

Commentary: The Conferees noted that, in other debates on informational privacy, two models of enforcement mechanisms have generally been proposed: one model sets up statutory standards of fair information practices and relies on civil suits by data subjects to implement them; the other sets up an administrative agency with the power to regulate (and possibly to license) the entire spectrum of information systems, and the power to order violators to cease and desist. *The Conferees supported overwhelmingly a proposal that both of these models be incorporated into a single piece of legislation.*

On the more difficult question of specifying the precise powers of a federal administrative agency, the Conferees reached no consensus. As discussed previously, the problems of defining "relevant" data collection for a wide variety of decision-makers seemed to require the flexibility and expertise of an agency with broad substantive rule-making powers. But a number of Conferees were hesitant about granting a federal agency such authority. Many individuals felt they needed further information to make a wise decision on this issue.

---

1. Dr. Edward J. Bloustein suggested that provision for counsel fees would fall outside the traditional practice of not providing these fees. He said: "I disagree, unless provision for counsel fees is provided on a much wider range of issues."

In the one discussion group which debated the character of the proposed administrative agency in great detail, the results were mixed. The group supported, by a large majority, an agency with strong investigatory and adjudicatory powers, and with the power to act on behalf of an individual or class of individuals whose rights have been impaired. But the group was evenly divided on granting the agency substantive rule-making powers; and the group overwhelmingly defeated a proposal that the agency should license all computerized information systems. The Conference went on record as supporting almost unanimously the need for a federal agency to oversee the code of fair information practices, but abstained on the questions of detail.

RECOMMENDATION XIX

No person should be compelled to divulge his Social Security number, unless expressly required to do so by federal law.

(Adopted by nearly unanimous vote)

Commentary: The use of the Social Security number as a universal identifier, and thus as an efficient means of file linkage, has been an important issue in various recent debates about informational privacy. It was recognized that, to some people, the number has also become an emotionally-charged symbol of what they view as the march toward an impersonal, conformist society.

The Conferees intend this Recommendation to apply to any organization, public or private, and to prevent that organization from conditioning any benefit or relationship on the disclosure of the Social Security number, i.e. to prevent all coercive requests.

Some discussion did reveal the need for individual identification procedures within information systems that are adequate to ensure the proper linking of data to the correct data subject: technically, this might imply the need for individual identifier numbers within information systems. Such a need should not be equated, however, with the present universality of the Social Security number, nor to improper linkage across systems made possible by individual identifier numbers.

REFLECTIONS ON SIX YEARS OF
LEGITIMATED ELECTRONIC SURVEILLANCE

by Herman Schwartz
Professor of Law, State University of New York at Buffalo

Watergate and wiretapping—they even *sound* similar! Rarely have we seen so many ironies, so many boomerangs, so many turnabouts as we have in the last two years, and most of these have resulted from electronic surveillance. The President taps his own brother; Henry Kissinger taps his own staff, the President's secret taping apparatus is used against him; E. Howard Hunt and G. Gordon Liddy reportedly taped their conversations with high White House officials, including the President.[1] The Nixon Supreme Court strikes down the Nixon claim to inherent power to tap dangerous people, in an opinion written by a justice who only the summer before defended the claim; the same Nixon Supreme Court, with four members chosen because of their hostility to letting criminals go free, issues a unanimous ruling on a nonconstitutional technicality that will probably result in the freeing of over 600 alleged criminals because the Department of Justice misrepresented to the courts that John Mitchell had personally seen and approved wiretap applications when he hadn't. And these are only some examples.

It is no surprise that wiretapping and electronic spying have played such a major role in these events. As I will develop later, wiretapping is essentially an instrument of war, used for intelligence purposes primarily. Unlike the more conventional police techniques, it is not really an effective crime detection device, but rather a technique for waging war. And no previous Administration, right from its first days in office, has seen the world, including fellow-Americans, in such war-like terms. "Enemies lists," "national security," "war on crime," "war on narcotics"—the militarist, beleaguered, state-of-siege attitudes reflected in these phrases and concepts are the distinguishing marks of the Nixon Administration.

The Nixon Administration does not, of course, have a monopoly of spying on its enemies. Franklin Delano Roosevelt, one of the most revered names in the liberal pantheon, formally authorized warrantless national security surveillance in 1940; Robert F. Kennedy may well have been the primary influence in legitimating wiretapping for law-enforcement purposes, though it appears that he ultimately changed his mind; Lyndon B. Johnson apparently listened in on newsmen's calls from the White House, according to a *New York Times* story a while back; governments in France and Italy have also used wiretapping against political and ideological enemies. But as former Nixon speechwriter William Safire put it vividly a few weeks ago, "the willingness to listen in ... to penetrate personal privacy in order to preserve national secrecy, was second nature to Richard Nixon ... [He has] an addiction to eavesdropping"[2]—which apparently goes for John Mitchell, too, as we shall see.

What I should like to do in this paper is (1) track the history of how we came to where we are today, including a discussion of the enactment of the Wiretap Act in 1968; (2) analyze some of the costs and benefits of electronic surveillance for law enforcement purposes, as revealed by the official statistics for six years of wiretapping under the Act, and by facts gleaned from court cases and elsewhere; (3) set forth some thoughts on national security surveillance; (4) offer some reflections on what all this means with respect to the value of electronic surveillance for law enforcement, for national security, and to the national temper and attitude; and finally (5) outline some possible remedies.

I. HOW WE GOT WHERE WE ARE

Several elements recur in the history of the wiretap controversy: (1) electronic surveillance is used primarily for victimless crimes like gambling and prostitution offenses; (2) its usage rises in a period of severe internal discord; (3) people become fearful of crime waves; and (4) the Supreme Court is deeply involved.

All of these were present in the 1920's, the first and still one of the most significant wiretap decades. There had, of course, been a good deal of private and public tapping earlier. The first federal tap was apparently installed in 1908, when Attorney General Bonaparte allowed his newly-created Bureau of Investigation—which later became the Federal Bureau of Investigation (FBI)—to tap in labor and immigration matters. There was apparently a good deal of private wiretapping in the newspaper wars early in the century, as well as local police surveillance of unions and even priests; the latter occurring in New York which was, then as now, the wiretap capital of the nation.

The 1919-31 and the 1961-72 periods seem the most significant and contain striking parallels. Enforcement of the liquor laws then and the narcotic and gambling and drug laws today have impelled law enforcement officials to use electronic surveillance extensively, for where there are no complainants, the need to infiltrate with either human or electronic spies seems essential. In both instances, as now seems clear, this has been carried out with very little impact. The "Red scares" of the 1920's, and the occurrence of some bombings (the perpetrators of which were never identified) are paralleled to the recent history of attacks on dissenters against the Vietnam War and black militants, and the accompanying violence and bombings. In both periods, there were abuses of the civil rights of political and ideological opponents, including break-ins, raids, abuses of grand juries, and a general indifference to legal limitations by law enforcement. It was during the early '20's that J. Edgar Hoover started his massive card index system of dissenters and dissidents, with Attorney General A. Mitchell Palmer's support. Congressmen and other political opponents were reportedly tapped, in a premonition of Watergate.

In 1924, when Harlan Stone took over the U.S. Justice Department in the wake of the Teapot Dome scandal, he banned all wiretapping, and Hoover went along, calling the practice "unethical." The U.S. Treasury Department also officially opposed surveillance at that time, just as the Internal Revenue Service (IRS) did in the '60's, but in both periods it quietly engaged in widespread surveillance.

In 1927, the Supreme Court gave a constitutional green light to electronic surveillance in the *Olmstead* case.[3] The decision is now only a constitutional relic, but in its time—and that time ran 40 years—it exercised a great and pernicious influence on the development of control of electronic surveillance. Its archaic requirement, that a trespass be committed before the Fourth Amendment was involved, meant that there was no protection against any bugging, and only the feeblest statutory protection against wiretapping.

The thirty years from 1930-1960 saw a great deal of federal, local and private wiretapping and bugging, the application to wiretapping of a prohibitory statute (§605 of the Communications Act) that seems to have been intended primarily for other purposes, and the revival of very extensive surveillance for intelligence and national security purposes. This time the surveillance was on authority from FDR in 1940[4] but it expanded far beyond his authority by later Presidents and Attorneys General to include, for example, organized crime. After the Supreme Court's construction of §605 of the Communications Act of 1934 to prohibit official as well as private wiretapping, numerous efforts were made in almost every Congress to override that decision, some of which came very close to succeeding. In 1940, Attorney General Robert H. Jackson found a way to get around it by ruling that the prohibition applied only to *both* interception and divulgence and that, so long as the fruits of a wiretap were not disclosed outside the Department, federal agents could continue to intercept.

In information released by Senator Hugh Scott (R-Pa.) last summer in an effort to show that the Nixon Administration has not used wiretapping more than other Administrations, it was revealed that from 1945-47, 1,257 national security wiretaps were installed. It appears also that throughout this period, local police wiretapped extensively both for themselves and for the FBI. There were frequent revelations of electronic surveillance throughout the country during this period, in articles by the National Lawyers' Guild as a result of revelations in the *Judith Coplon* case, by Alan Westin, by the *Reporter* magazine, and in Samuel Dash's monumental study published in the late '50's, *The Eavesdroppers.*

In 1957, there occurred an event which was to transform the situation: the meeting at Apalachin, New York of alleged organized crime figures, which was broken up by New York State Police. Law enforcement authorities now felt they had convincing proof of a massive organized crime conspiracy. J. Edgar Hoover had earlier resisted efforts to bring the Bureau into that area, either because he feared corruption or doubted that he would be able to rack up impressive statistics. After Apalachin, however, he began to tap and bug to make up for lost time.

Perhaps most importantly, Robert F. Kennedy, then a counsel for Senator John McClellan's rackets committee, became convinced that organized crime was one of America's greatest threats. In 1961, he became Attorney General and turned the full force of his enormous abilities and power against organized crime.[5] The IRS was recruited and Commissioner Mortimer Caplin wrote his staff:

> I cannot emphasize too strongly the importance I attach to the success of the Service's contribution to this over-all program ... The tax returns of major racketeers to be identified by the Department of Justice will be subjected to the "saturation type" investigation, utilizing such manpower on each case as can be efficiently employed. In conducting such investigations, full use will be made of available electronic equipment and other technical aids as well as such investigative techniques as surveillance, undercover work, etc.[6]

Urged strongly by Kennedy to use "technical equipment," the significance of which everyone understood, Hoover intensified tapping and bugging. Although there is a good deal of dispute as to how much Kennedy knew about the microphone bugs, which Hoover justified under a 1954 Herbert Brownell memorandum on internal security, it is undisputed that Hoover engaged in almost as much bugging as tapping. A letter from Assistant Attorney General Miller in May, 1961, reported that the FBI had 67 bugs and some 85 taps in operation as of the date of the testimony; this amounts to some unknown multiple of these for the whole year, since obviously some of these 67 bugs and 85 taps were removed during the year and others installed elsewhere. In 1965, when Attorney General Nicholas deB. Katzenbach tried to force Hoover to terminate these bugs—almost all of which were patently illegal because they generally involved break-ins—Hoover responded that 99% of his organized crime program

involved these bugs and Katzenbach allowed Hoover to phase them out over a six-month period.

Many of these taps and bugs were in for lengthy periods of time—the Maggadino tapes in Buffalo ran to 76,000 pages; the de Cavalcante surveillance lasted four years. Kennedy treated the whole business very casually—he kept no records or review of his authorizations, and the first such effort was made by Ramsey Clark. (Attorneys John Shattuck and Leon Friedman have documented the continuing laxity in the recordkeeping on national security surveillance in their April 24, 1974 congressional testimony.)

We have been told that little of this tapping and bugging was aimed at getting information for specific criminal prosecutions; rather it was gathered primarily for intelligence. That point was made clear by some of the organized crime specialists like G. Robert Blakey, one of the chief draftsmen of what became the 1968 Wiretap Act, who told a congressional committee in 1967:

> The normal criminal situation deals with an incident, a murder, a rape, or a robbery, probably committed by one person. The criminal investigation normally moves from the known crime toward the unknown criminal. This is in sharp contrast to the type of procedures you must use in the investigation of organized crime. Here in many situations you have known criminals but unknown crimes.

> So it is necessary to subject the known criminals to surveillance, that is, to monitor their activities. It is necessary to identify their criminal and noncriminal associates; it is necessary to identify their areas of operation, both legal and illegal. Strategic intelligence attempts to paint this broad, overall picture of the criminal's activities in order that an investigator can ultimately move in with a specific criminal investigation and prosecution ... Perhaps the best illustration I can give you is the "airtels" ... [which] represent the gathering of strategic intelligence against organized crime in that case against Raymond Patriarca.

> Tactical intelligence, on the other hand, is illustrated by the *Osborn* case, which the Supreme Court heavily relied upon in the

Berger opinion. You moved in there and monitored only one conversation or only one meeting. You had a limited, tactical purpose, whereas in the Patriarca situation you had a broader purpose ... So the distinction deals, first, with the purpose of the agency and then perhaps, second, with the extent of time the subject is under surveillance.[7]

Ramsey Clark and others disparaged the value of what was obtained from such "strategic intelligence" techniques. But in the early and middle 1960's few people listened. Organized crime had become the anti-Christ, and Robert Kennedy was leading the Inquisition.

In 1961, Kennedy introduced a bill to permit official wiretapping though he explicitly excluded bugging on the ground that, as Assistant Attorney General Herbert S. Miller put it, the issue "with all its ramifications" needed to be "carefully explored" before legislation was enacted.[8] Whether this statement was made disingenuously or otherwise, the fact remains that during this period the FBI was operating an enormous number of microphone surveillances.

Pressure for the legitimation of wiretapping came from other sources as well. The President's Crime Commission issued its report in 1967, and near the top of its priorities was organized crime. Influenced heavily by attorneys from Kennedy's Organized Crime Section, the Commission ascribed to organized crime virtually all the ills of the body politic. And while it did not recommend the legitimation of wiretapping—though a majority of the Commission did endorse this—the message was clear. The ABA got on the bandwagon, led by Federal Court of Appeals Judge J. Edward Lumbard, a former prosecutor and the chief judicial proponent of police tapping. Donald Cressey, one of America's leading criminologists, was also converted and wrote angrily, "If organized criminals could be handled as enemies of war, rather than as citizens with the rights of due process, they could have been wiped out long ago."[9] Apart from the rather cavalier attitude toward guilt, innocence, and the rights of fellow Americans as reflected in Cressey's comment, the fact is that "organized criminals" have been treated as "enemies of war," as Victor Navasky's book makes clear, but with little success in wiping them out.

The pressures were not entirely one-sided however. In the mid-1960's, the enormous amount of illegal electronic surveillance by the FBI, IRS, and others suddenly came to light when an FBI bug was accidentally discovered in a Las Vegas gambler's office and in Washington's Sheraton-Carlton hotel where, as in so many other instances, lawyer-client conversations were overheard. This led to a series of court-ordered revelations of illegal federal surveillance involving some 50 or more cases. (The pattern of accidental discovery of official illegality with respect to wiretapping leading to a loss of prosecutions, which started with the *Coplon* case, has just been repeated in the series of cases culminating in *United States v. Giordano,* where 626 defendants in some 60 cases will automatically go free because of official impropriety.) As a result, President Johnson ordered an end to all electronic surveillance except in national security cases.

At the same time, Senator Edward V. Long began to hold hearings on illegal surveillance by other federal agencies. His investigation discovered, for example, that despite a 1938 Treasury directive banning electronic surveillance, IRS agents tapped and bugged promiscuously, set up some 24 bugged conference rooms, and engaged in breaking and entering—all with an arrogance reflected in the statement of one agent that everything was justified in the battle against criminals.[10] Moreover, the IRS conducted a school in Washington, D.C., to which agents came to learn electronic surveillance and lock-picking and from which experts were sent out to install and remove equipment.

Other agencies were also disclosed to have tapped and bugged widely. One Federal Bureau of Narcotics agent testified that he had broken into homes "hundreds of times" in the 1950's to install microphone surveillances.[11] If caught, he reported, his instructions were to deny that he had been authorized to do so by his superiors—even though he had.

The Federal Drug Administration (FDA), the post office, and other federal agencies were similarly exposed. In short, America was presented with a picture of government agents tapping and bugging thousands upon thousands of Americans in knowing and flagrant violation of the law, and often in equally gross violation of constitutional and other privileges—all usually to very little avail. In Kansas

City, Missouri, it was found that a "saturation drive" against organized crime involving 135 agents and at least $2 million had netted only three convictions, for which the three defendants received sentences of six months, four months, and three months—what Senator Edward V. Long derisively called "minnows."

During these hearings, bugs in martini olives, cigarette packs and other unlikely spots were demonstrated. Shortly thereafter, the President sent up a bill proposed by his Attorney General, Ramsey Clark, to bar virtually all wiretapping.

At this time, in the mid-1960's, the Supreme Court entered the picture decisively and, in the *Berger* and *Katz* cases,[12] set out the contours of a constitutional wiretap statute by approving in principle a gambling wiretap in *Katz*, while striking down the New York wiretap statute in *Berger* as too loose. In the course of its *Katz* decision, the Supreme Court finally overruled the *Olmstead* trespass doctrine. Later, in June, 1968, electronic surveillance was finally legitimated with the passage of Title III of the Omnibus Crime Control and Safe Streets Act of 1968.

The story of the enactment of this legislation has been brilliantly told by Richard Harris in the December 14, 1968 issue of the *New Yorker*. It is enough to say here that, when President Johnson signed the bill legitimating electronic surveillance, Robert Kennedy was dead, but his ghost hovered over the event. It was he who had stimulated the drive against organized crime which fueled the demand for wiretapping, and it was his assassination that propelled the bill out of the House Judiciary Committee where Chairman Celler had hoped to bottle it up. Adding to the irony was the fact that Kennedy had long since lost interest in the organized crime drive and was against the bill. Moreover, the statute was enacted while Ramsey Clark was Attorney General—the only Attorney General since Stone opposed to wiretapping.

These ironies reflected the frailty, if not the impotence, of the liberal tradition in America in a period of crisis. Americans were frightened as rarely before in a time of official peace: they feared street crime, black rebellions, radicals, young people, organized crime. Hanging over everything was Vietnam.

Congress had a pretty good idea of how bad the bill was. As Richard Harris reported, "all those who voted against it, many of those who voted for it, and most of those who didn't vote at all [believed] the bill was a piece of demagoguery, devised out of malevolence and enacted in hysteria." Nevertheless, records Harris, "in the House, only seventeen members voted against it, and in the Senate only four."

II. WHAT WE HAVE:
STATUTORY AND EXECUTIVE AUTHORITY

A. The Statute

Wiretapping and bugging are done under two forms of authority, the second of which has not yet been approved by the Supreme Court: (1) law enforcement surveillance under Title III of the Omnibus Crime Control and Safe Streets Act of 1968,[13] which requires prior judicial approval; and (2) surveillance for national security purposes which is done upon merely executive approval.

Only law enforcement surveillance is subject to the restrictions (such as they are) of the 1968 Act. And despite the length and complexity of the statute, the restrictions are not very severe. But first, a few words about the facial structure of the Act.

In form, the law bars *all* interceptions of communication except in certain specifically defined classes: (1) if done by law enforcement officials, pursuant to a warrant issued by a court and subject to certain restrictions; (2) eavesdropping with the consent of one of the parties to the conversation; and (3) certain special situations involving telephone company and business monitoring. Illegally-obtained wiretapping is not usable in any official proceeding, and damages for illegal surveillance are possible. States that wish to do so may pass legislation similar to the federal act to allow their police to use electronic surveillance.

The preamble promised that electronic surveillance would be used sparingly and only for serious crimes, and that individual privacy would receive greater protection than before because of the various provisions prohibiting and/or limiting use of the technique, and the provisions of the Act would be enforced.

It hasn't worked out that way.

• Wiretapping has been used very extensively, largely and deliberately for minor offenses like gambling and against small-time operators.

• The conversations of vast numbers of people, many of them totally innocent of any crime, have been overheard—often in surveillances lasting for very long periods of time.

• Few convictions have resulted, and rarely for anything more than gambling and some narcotics cases. Even in some of these cases, there are indications that the wiretap evidence played a minor or negligible role in the prosecution.

• Many of the "protections" of the act have been annulled by judge-shopping, statutory loopholes, and improper execution. There have been almost no successful damage actions to date for illegal wiretapping—though this may change—and very few prosecutions.

On top of all this, we have recently learned of the huge number of Americans eavesdropped upon in the name of national security, without any judicial controls, because President Richard Nixon and Attorney General John Mitchell thought them "dangerous."

Much of this was predictable and was, in fact, predicted. Indeed, almost all commentators have condemned the act as unconstitutional under *Katz* and *Berger,* but so far, all the appellate courts and all but one district court—and that one was quickly reversed—have found the Act constitutional. Nevertheless, the facial defects of the statute are many. For example:

• It deliberately allows virtually indefinite periods of listening, because it allows extensions, even if nothing is found so long as there is a reasonable excuse for failure to come up with something—even though the *Berger* court condemned 60-day taps as too long.[14]

• It draws no distinction between tapping and bugging despite the vastly more pernicious nature of the latter—one can avoid using the phone in many situations, but how does one avoid bugs in one's home or office? Even Nixon had problems here, even though he authorized the bugs himself. It will be recalled that in the early '60's, the proposed bills excluded bugging, but the crime-busters were in command in 1968 and they obviously grabbed everything they could.

• The Act allows judge-shopping without any

limitation. In consequence, only five or six applications for either initial authorization or an extension have been turned down in the six years of the operation of the Act; in New Jersey, for example, the second state most prolific in wiretapping next to New York, a Mercer County judge named Frank Klingfield has never refused an application. In 1972 he issued 134, or one-sixth of the national total. In Erie and Niagara counties in New York—where there are many judges available—one judge issued thirteen out of the fourteen 1971 orders, and in 1970 he issued eight out of nine Erie County orders and all ten Niagara County orders. Many of these have been suppressed in federal and state courts as improperly issued or executed. In Albany County, one judge issued twelve out of fourteen 1971 orders. A similar situation holds true elsewhere, such as in Florida and Baltimore, Maryland.

• The Act is not limited to serious crimes, but allows tapping for a laundry list of federal offenses and an almost open-ended list of state offenses—including gambling, marijuana, and any State offense with a penalty of one year or more.[15]

• The Act makes no substantial effort to limit the surveillance to expectedly criminal conversations, but allows a broad definition of what may be intercepted. As a result, there is overwhelming statistical evidence that the bulk of the conversations overheard are innocent. It is not unlikely, moreover, judging by certain individual situations that have come to light, that the statistics in question—which are provided by the prosecutor and therefore can contain all the vices of self-reporting now so well documented from our experience with the FBI's Uniform Crime Reports—are substantially understated.

These are just some of the facially-obvious problems with the statute. One of the relatively useful provisions in the statute required prosecutors and judges to file reports about the use of Title III wiretaps, and for all the definitional and other shortcomings of this procedure, the statistics tell us some things about the costs and benefits of court-authorized surveillance. Although statistics have been issued for 1968-1973, the 1973 data has not yet been fully analyzed in detail. The figures will therefore be only approximate, but are probably fairly accurate.

B. The Results as Reflected in the Statistics:
Volume of Surveillance

In the first place, the statistics document that far from being a rare device to be used only for such serious offenses as homicide, kidnapping and espionage, electronic surveillance has become a routine technique used primarily in gambling cases. Other sources indicate that it is used largely against small-time operators. Indeed, there seems to have been a deliberate campaign against small gamblers named "Project Anvil"; a recent interview with FBI personnel, discussed below, supports this.

The statistics show that in the 1968-1973 period,[16] almost 3,500 taps and bugs were authorized and installed, and almost 160,000 people were reported to have been overheard in more than 2.1 million conversations. Of these, about 48,000 people were overheard on federal taps and bugs authorized by a court order—national security taps *not* included—and some 76,000 on state taps. It is not clear that the state figure includes 76,000 different people, although the federal figure purportedly does try to avoid duplication. The overwhelming proportion of the state tapping was found to be in New York and New Jersey, with most of it in New York. In 1973, for example, New York accounted for 46% of all surveillance and New Jersey for 30%. This is a slight decline from prior years where the two states generally accounted for 80-85% of the total, with New York always accounting for the lion's share.

The following figures tell the story:

AUTHORIZED AND INSTALLED WIRETAPS BY YEAR

Year	Combined Federal and State			
	Orders	Installations	People	Conversations
1968 (6 mos)	174	167	4,250	62,291
1969	302	290	14,656	186,229
1970	597	590	25,812	373,763
1971	816	792	32,509	496,629
1972	855	839	42,182	517,205
1973	866	812	39,788*	495,320*
Totals	3,610	3,490	159,197*	2,131,437*

*These figures are preliminary, in that they are derived from over-all averages reported by the Administrative Office. The exact figures, obtained by analyzing the reports on each individual wiretap and bug, are generally close to these averages.

Perhaps the most troublesome aspect of this massive attack on individual privacy is that, as mentioned before, almost none of it is for serious crimes like homicide, kidnapping, and espionage, but most of it is for gambling and to a rather lesser extent for drugs. The following table tells that story:

FEDERAL AND STATE ELECTRONIC SURVEILLANCE BY YEAR[a]

Year	Gambling	Drugs	Homocide	Kidnap	Other	Total
			Federal Installations			
1969	20	4	0	1	5	30
1970	120	39	0	0	21	180
1971	248	21	0	0	12	281
1972	147	35	0	0	23	205
1973	81	28	0	0	21	130
Totals	616	127	0	1	82	826
			State Installations			
1968	18	68	20	1	60	167
1969	78	80	19	1	82	260
1970	204	84	20	0	95+7[b]	410
1971	304	104	18	1	84	511
1972	340	193	33	0	68	634
1973[c]	365	201	47	2	119	734
Totals	1,309	730	157[d]	5	508+7[b]	2,716

[a] These figures are drawn directly from the individual reports appearing in the Appendix to the Report issued by the Administrative Office of the United States Court, submitted to that Office by prosecutors and judges.

[b] Offense not indicated.

[c] The 1973 figures are slightly overstated, for they are based on the *authorized* surveillances, which exceeds the number actually installed by a slight amount. It has not yet been possible to determine the exact number of installed state surveillances, for there are certain lacunae in the reports. The differences between authorized and installed are, however, relatively small.

[d] The "homicide" figures are greatly inflated, for they include not just murder, but conspiracy, attempts, threats, solicitations, as well as assaults. Why the latter are lumped in with "murder" is not clear.

Most of this surveillance has gone on for considerable periods of time. Federal eavesdropping has averaged 13.5 days, which is less than the 60 days considered excessive by the Supreme Court in the *Berger* case, but still a high average, given the fact that these instruments are usually in continuous operation every minute of those days. State officials have observed no such time limitations. In 1968, 32 out of 167 state surveillance devices operated for 60 or more days—three for as long as 100 to 199 days. In 1969, over 20 percent operated for 60 or more days, and four transmitted continuously for 200 days. A similar pattern has continued through 1972, when 42 lasted for 60 or more days. Of course, the statute, if one reads it carefully, tacitly permits, and indeed, contemplates such severe intrusions. As noted above, it allows an indefinite number of extensions, *even if nothing fruitful has developed,* so long as there is some explanation for the failure to overhear anything useful.

As a result, from 1968 to 1973 the courts granted 1,323 extensions on about 3,492 installations. The Senate Committee Report accompanying the bill cites, as an example of what the statute allows, a 1955 California case which involved continuous surveillance for over 15 months. (When Senator Hiram Fong pointed out in debate over the bill that it held the possibility of indefinite surveillance, Senator John McClellan, the bill's floor manager, did not deny it.)

Such lengthy continuous surveillance might be barely tolerable if we knew that nothing but criminal activity were being overheard, but such a limitation is practically impossible. Although the statute explicitly requires that investigators minimize the interception of irrelevant, innocent conversations, this is virtually a technical and administrative impossibility, as the reports of wiretapped conversations document. Critics of wiretapping and bugging have stressed the inherently unlimited nature of this technique, and the experience under the Act supports this criticism. More than a few cases have shown that the statutory mandate of minimization has been disregarded by both judges and investigators.

According to the reporting prosecutors' own definition and evaluation, an enormously high percentage of overheard conversations are not "incriminating," whatever the precise definition of that word. On the state level, for example, the *non-incriminating* conversations that were overheard ranged from 78 percent to 70 percent between 1968 and 1970. In 1971-72, that figure dropped, as the states began to concentrate more on gambling, but the figure still remained near 50 percent. The 1973 figures haven't been calculated yet.

At the federal level, the non-incriminating conversations comprised about 18 percent of the total in 1969, but rose to 40 percent in 1972. Even these figures seem understated, for at least one federal court has found that, although federal prosecutors reported that 85 percent of a group of overheard conversations were incriminating, in fact, only five to ten percent were.[17] More importantly perhaps, once we move away from gambling cases—the proportion of incriminating conversations in gambling cases is necessarily and unusually high because the phones are generally used exclusively for the gambling operation—the proportion of innocent conversations overheard is well over *80 percent.*

The large number of wiretap installations for petty gambling in the federal, New York, and New Jersey systems indicates it is not being used sparingly. Moreover, the recent decision by the Supreme Court in *United States v. Giordano,* _____ U.S. _____ , (May 13, 1974), indicates that, contrary to Attorney General Mitchell's claims,[18] he never even saw the application to which his approval was initialed.

Moreover, the statutory requirements in §2518(4)(e), that the interception end when the conversations sought are first obtained unless the court orders otherwise, seems to be observed by many judges who simply order routinely "otherwise." Thus, although the Supreme Court seemed to intend that electronic surveillance be subject to more restrictions than a conventional search, the statute provides less.

Finally, it appears clear that the statutory requirement in §2518(3)(c), that the order issue only if normal investigative procedures haven't worked, won't work or are too dangerous, is not being enforced very stringently. Even the one judge hostile to wiretapping held that the burden on the government in this regard is not very great.[19]

These factors only point up the frailty of the reed on which individual privacy has been made to depend—the court order system. With respect to conventional search warrants, judicial supervision is of only limited help, since many judges see themselves merely as the judicial branch of law enforcement operations. Former District Attorney of Philadelphia Arlen Specter, an opponent of law enforcement wiretapping, has put the matter somewhat more delicately;

> Judges tend to rely upon the prosecutor . . .
> Experience in our criminal courts has shown the prior judicial approval for search and seizure warrants is more a matter of form than of substance in guaranteeing the existence of probable cause to substantiate the need for a search. . . . Some judges have specifically said they do not want to know the reasons for the tap so that they could not be accused later of relaying the information to men suspected of organized crime activities.

So we find wiretapping routinely available to federal and state prosecutors (the latter, of course, only in states with wiretap statutes) who want to spend the money. And it takes a lot of money. The average federal tap in 1973 cost $12,236 and in prior years, the average cost for a drug case installation was over $60,000. The state figures purport to be much lower, but are so incomplete and inconsistent as to be worthless. Moreover, even these figures are grossly understated in both the state and federal reports, for they include only the hardware and investigators' and transcribers' time, and omit a very substantial amount of lawyers' and judges' time in preparing and evaluating the applications for permission to tap and bug, to say nothing of the cost of the suppression hearings.

C. The Results: Successful Prosecutions

Measured by the rate of convictions, it is hard to call electronic surveillance much of a success. It is not used very much for anything but gambling, and many of the most important urban states—California, Illinois, Pennsylvania, Michigan, and Ohio—have not even bothered to accept Congress' invitation to allow their police to tap and bug. As of December, 1973, 29 states did not feel this was a worthwhile technique; of those that allow police wiretapping and bugging, five did not even bother to use that authority in 1973.

Moreover, the single most significant wiretapping jurisdiction—the federal establishment—cut its usage from 210 in 1972 to 130 in 1973—a drop of over 35% in one year; this, in turn, followed a drop from 281 in 1971 to 210 in 1972, a drop of 25%, or a drop of over 50% in the two years from 1971-1973. This sharp drop may be attributable to the departure of Attorney General John Mitchell from the Justice Department in early 1972 to operate Committee to Re-elect the President (CREEP), for the drop coincided with that departure. It does indicate that, as some have concluded, electronic surveillance is simply not worth the cost. The official FBI explanation, as reported in an Associated Press story on May 21, 1974, is that the FBI has decided to switch "from quantity to quality," and will henceforth refrain from going after the " 'mom and pop' bookies who are not directly tied into the crime syndicate." [20]

The picture as to convictions, purportedly resulting from electronic eavesdropping in those jurisdictions which do wiretap, is still not complete. It apparently takes some 22.5 months to fully process a federal case, so the only reliable results that I have had a chance to analyze fully are for 1969 and 1970. I have, however, made a preliminary survey of the 1971 surveillances and will include that here. Moreover, there is a very difficult question of causality: even where wiretapping was used in a case, how closely related was it to whatever results were achieved? In more than a few cases, courts and prosecutors have commented on the irrelevance of the wiretap evidence. In one state case, the prosecutor himself reported that the conviction was not obtained from the tap. In many cases involving the disclosure of illegal taps, federal prosecutors have argued that whatever wiretapping was done did not produce any of the evidence used at the trial.

Finally, there is the question of appeals and reversals. Many federal convictions will be overturned or are in jeopardy because of the *Giordano* case, and this particularly affects the 1969-70 interceptions, since the Justice Department's procedures were tightened up afterwards.

Even without this rather special set of reservations, the figures still show very thin results indeed.. For 1969-71, only 1,037 persons were convicted as a result of 491 federal wiretaps despite the expenditure of at least $4.5 million on the electronic surveillances alone. A more interesting figure is that, of the 210 federal taps installed in 1969-70, only 67, or nearly a third, were related to a conviction. This means that 143 federal installations resulted in little or nothing.

Most of the convictions were for gambling and drugs: of the 1,037 persons convicted, 828 were for those two offenses—643 for gambling and 185 for drugs. More importantly, my check of some of these cases indicates that many, if not most, of these gamblers seem to be small operators, and a recent study provides some support for this conclusion.[21] FBI Director Hoover opposed the federal anti-gambling law because it dealt with what was essentially "a function of local law enforcement."[22] This concern with "local law enforcement" seems to have reflected a deliberate policy which has now been abandoned as useless.

Gambling is, of course, supposed to be the lifeblood of organized crime, and perhaps these few gambling convictions led to something much bigger. But apparently the FBI has finally decided that things haven't worked out that way. Indeed, most experts are agreed that organized crime, whatever it is, has not been weakened very much.

The arrest figures are, of course, much higher—about 1,400 federal arrests in 1969-70 as opposed to 550 convictions. But the arrest figure is far less significant. For one thing, most arrests do *not* result in convictions. And under the statute, a wiretap order is not authorized unless there is already probable cause to believe that the suspect is committing a crime, which is the same standard that is required for an arrest. In other words, even before the wiretap is installed, there should be enough evidence to arrest someone. It is, therefore, difficult to know how much the tap contributed, if at all, to any arrests. And even with respect to arrests, in 1969-70 over one-third of the federal wiretap installations did not result in an arrest.

The state results are even more meager: 1,597 convictions in the five and one-half years. Again the 1969-70 figures are the most complete,[23] and they tell almost the same story as the federal. For 670 surveillances installed during that period, only 870 people were convicted at a reported cost of about $1.4 million, with 520, or 60%, in gambling cases, even though gambling accounted for only 282

installations, or about 40%. Drug offenses, probably including marijuana, accounted for another 128. More importantly, only about a third of the installations were related to any convictions.

Not only did 28 states not consider electronic eavesdropping crucial enough to law enforcement to pass the appropriate enabling legislation, but even those that did give their police this authority used it very rarely—except for New York and New Jersey. In 1972, for example, all 19 other states with authorization installed only about 125 taps and bugs out of the 634 total. Perhaps there are reasons other than its lack of utility, but at first blush, it would seem that a crucial investigative device would be employed more often.

Doubts as to the value of wiretapping and bugging come not just from these figures, but from other sources. Many of the Strike Forces created to fight organized crime don't use electronic eavesdropping very much, if at all, as the *New York Times* report on various prosecutors' reaction to the *Giordano* decision indicated. One Strike Force prosecutor told author Edith Lapidus:

It has not often been applicable. We have been able to make a case without it and we have had more indictments and convictions than any Strike Force in the country.[24]

A New York prosecutor specializing in drug cases told *The Wall Street Journal* that its importance in such cases was greatly overrated. A random survey that I had a student make of major successful prosecutions in corruption, drugs and other areas, as reported in the *New York Times* from July 1, 1972, through June 30, 1973, disclosed very little electronic surveillance in any but a few cases; and, in the few, it was usually consent surveillance involving a wired informer rather than the more conventional wiretapping.

While attorney Henry Petersen of the U.S. Justice Department tried to provide Senator McClellan with data to show the importance of wiretapping and the gambling laws in convicting organized crime leaders, his figures showed mostly indictments only. Very few leaders, and relatively few convictions, related to the wiretaps.[25]

This lack of utility for crime-solving comes as no surprise, for it flows directly from the fact that wiretapping and bugging are really tools of *strategic intelligence,* not crime detection. And the payoff on intelligence is, at best, long-term and indirect, and in many instances, very small. Indeed, although one cannot be sure, it does seem as if law enforcement has not been able to get the kind of intelligence that would prevent gangland killings, for example, or head off other unfortunate events.

A type of electronic surveillance that does seem valuable and which I personally find compatible with the Fourth Amendment under proper restrictions is consent surveillance. It seems clear that the use of wired informers is both necessary and helpful; whatever use electronic devices have in extortion and kidnapping cases seems to involve this kind of interception. Moreover, it can be limited with respect to time, space, people, etc. Indeed, all of the cases (except *Olmstead*) in which the Supreme Court sustained wiretapping involved a very precise and limited surveillance, and usually with the consent of one of the parties.[26]

But such surveillance should not be exempt from Fourth Amendment requirements, as the Supreme Court and the statute have done.[27] Consent surveillance is merely a specific instance of the general problems associated with police use of informers. In the past, police have resisted application of Fourth Amendment specificity standards to informers, partly because it is often difficult to specify the individual target—the informer is frequently told simply to infiltrate a group and to learn what he can. This difficulty has generally disappeared when electronic surveillance is introduced, for that is usually done when the police want to zero in on a specific target.

This is not to assert that electronic surveillance is of no value. We know too little to say that, and there probably have been at least a few instances where the information gained from the tap or bug has been very helpful. District Attorney Eugene Gold of Brooklyn, who has become one of the most avid wiretappers, claims to have "broken the back" of organized crime in Brooklyn with the tap in a trailer. Perhaps. So far, little seems to have come from that, but it is still early. Moreover, Gold apparently had Paul Vario, his chief target, on other charges already.

But social policy cannot be decided by a few examples in one way or another. The statistics and practice of the last six years cast serious doubts on the claims of the tappers, while the danger to liberty and invasions of privacy are indisputable.

III. NATIONAL SECURITY SURVEILLANCE

The statute creates a sharp distinction between court-authorized taps for crime detection and "national security" taps, which have been installed without antecedent judicial approval. In practice, the line has not been that sharp. In the name of national security, FBI Director Hoover installed hundreds of bugs in his fight against organized crime. As reporter Fred Graham has noted, FBI agents apparently had no difficulty justifying (to themselves, at least) a tap on a restaurant on the ground that the Mafia was a threat to "national security."[28]

The line became blurred even more when the Nixon Administration claimed authority to tap people whom it considered "dangerous" without any prior judicial approval, and with virtually negligible judicial review if the tap should come to light. In case after case, it ultimately appeared that, under the national security intelligence claim, tapping was done upon people being sought for prosecution, raising suspicions that the national security intelligence cover was being invoked to avoid complying with Title III.[29] However, in a startlingly libertarian decision for a unanimous Supreme Court (Justice Rehnquist abstaining), Justice Powell denied the government this authority where *domestic* intelligence was concerned in *United States v. U.S. Dist. Ct.,* 407 U.S. 297 (1972).

The decision has been so widely discussed that there is little need to elaborate on it. But there are a few extremely troubling loopholes in the opinion—very troubling indeed.

The first is that Justice Powell explicitly left open the possibility that a warrant for intelligence surveillance could be obtained under standards more relaxed than normal. Powell declared:

Moreover, we do not hold that the same type of standards and procedures prescribed by Title III are necessarily applicable to this case. We recognize that domestic security surveillance may involve different policy and practical considerations from the surveillance of "ordinary crime." The gathering of security intelligence is often long range and involves the interrelation of various sources and types of information. The exact targets of such surveillance may be more difficult to identify than in surveillance operations against many types of crime specified in Title III. Often, too, the emphasis of domestic intelligence gathering is on the prevention of unlawful activity or the enhancement of the Government's preparedness for some possible future crisis or emergency. Thus, the focus of domestic surveillance may be less precise than that directed against more conventional types of crime.

Given those potential distinctions between Title III criminal surveillances and those involving the domestic security, Congress may wish to consider protective standards for the latter which differ from those already prescribed for specified crimes in Title III. Different standards may be compatible with the Fourth Amendment if they are reasonable both in relation to the legitimate need of Government for intelligence information and the protected rights of our citizens. For the warrant application may vary according to the governmental interest to be enforced and the nature of citizen rights deserving protection [quoting *Camara*]. It may be that Congress, for example, would judge that the application and affidavit showing probable cause need not follow the exact requirements of §2518 but should allege other circumstances more appropriate to domestic security cases; that the request for prior court authorization could, in sensitive cases, be made to any member of a specially designated court (e.g., the District Court or Court of Appeals for the District of Columbia); and that the time and reporting requirements need not be so strict as those in §2518.

Such a warrant would seem to run directly counter to the long-established requirement of specificity in Fourth Amendment warrants, a requirement that the Supreme Court has said is the essence of the Fourth Amendment.[30] Moreover, the distinction between intelligence and prosecution is so thin, as experience demonstates, that it seems unworkable. The result can only be a further dilution of Fourth Amendment restrictions in conventional criminal prosecution, which would apply not just to electronic surveillance but to all other investigatory techniques.

Powell was here participating in the current Supreme Court's tendency to allow as "reasonable" every prosecutorial effort to dispense with fundamental Fourth Amendment limitations as to specificity, probable cause and scope of the search. This has been seen in many areas, such as area searches near the border, safekeeping of property, searches incident to arrest, stop and frisk,[31] and others. Fourth Amendment "reasonableness" is coming to mean little more than that the police come up with some reason, regardless of the Fourth amendment values and precedents the other way.

Initially, the Justice Department said it would not seek intelligence-seeking authorization of the kind suggested by Justice Powell. But in testimony just a few weeks ago, an FBI spokesman declared that such legislation is being prepared. Hopefully, Congress will reject it. The Fourth Amendment requirements are riddled with so many exceptions already, the standards for probable cause are so loose, judicial scrutiny is likely to be so lax where internal security or suspected violence is alleged, and our experience of abuses from such loose requirements is so bad, that this legislation should get nowhere.

The second loophole was opened by Powell when he explicitly limited the Court's condemnation of warrantless wiretapping to surveillance of *domestic* groups. The kind of link to foreign powers that will make the group not "domestic" is still uncertain. So far, indications are that the Justice Department construes "foreign" very broadly: it has sought to justify surveillance of both the Jewish Defense League and Morton Halperin, both indisputably domestic, as "foreign" surveillance, and it has been upheld by a district court with respect to the former.[32]

The volume of governmental electronic surveillance actually affected by the decision therefore remains unclear. The Department stated that it felt required to turn off only six taps, leaving 27 in operation, a surprisingly low figure if one assumes that the various embassy taps were unaffected. Another unsettling note appeared just a few weeks ago, when David Burnham of the *New York Times* stated that, sometime last August, **82** such taps were in operation, even though President Nixon had said in 1971 that there were to be no more than 50 in operation at any one time. Why the jump to 82 from 27 or even 50?

How much national security wiretapping has occurred in the past is also hard to estimate. Only recently have we obtained any statistics, and these are fragmentary and ambiguous.

In the first place the White House figures, released by Senator Hugh Scott and referred to earlier, show the following "national security wiretaps . . . subject to refinement as the detailed search proceeds."

1945 – 519	1959 – 120
1946 – 346	1960 – 115
1947 – 374	1961 – 140
1948 – 416	1962 – 198
1949 – 471	1963 – 244
1950 – 270	1964 – 260
1951 – 285	1965 – 233
1952 – 285	1966 – 174
1953 – 300	1967 – 113
1954 – 322	1968 – 82
1955 – 214	1969 – 123
1956 – 164	1970 – 102
1957 – 173	1971 – 101
1958 – 166	1972 – 108

(So far, there has been no refinement—the "detailed search" may have been derailed by other "detailed searches.")

These figures are probably understated. Because they refer to "national security *wiretaps*," it is not clear whether they include bugs. Also, it is most unlikely that they include military, CIA, and whatever local Red Squad surveillance was done on behalf of the FBI, of which there is some evidence. The recent information of 82 in one day in 1973 raises the possibility of a jump to several hundred for the year. Moreover, the figures do not disclose how many people and conversations were overheard.

We do have some information on the latter point from another source. Classified information supplied to Senator Edward Kennedy's staff indicates that from 1968 to 1970, the average

national security tap lasted from 78.3 to 290.7 days. This computation is confirmed by information that has come to light involving the cases of the Jewish Defense League and Morton Halperin. Since the federal taps have averaged about 56 people and 900 conversations per 13.5-day interception, simple arithmetic indicates that each individual federal national security tap caught between 5,500 and 15,000 people per year, and that the 100 annual taps of recent years overheard between 55,000 and 150,000 people per year!

Support for this huge figure comes from a few items of information that have come out of court cases. For example, in the Detroit Weathermen case, it has been reported that one tape contained 12,000 separate conversations, many of them involving lawyer-client conversations.

Except for such episodic disclosures, we have no systematic information as to the scope and extent of such national security surveillance.

The value of this surveillance has been disputed by highly-informed and experienced experts. In congressional testimony this past June, former Attorney General Ramsey Clark declared, "I have tried to estimate—I do not know that it is possible—the value of the [national security] taps that we have. I know that not one percent of the information that we have picked up has any possible use." When Senator Edward M. Kennedy asked, "What would be the impact on our national security if the Executive Branch were to eliminate all warrantless tapping at the present time," Clark replied, "I think the impact would be absolutely zero."[33]

Because this security surveillance is carried out secretly and solely by the Executive Branch, it has been completely unregulated. Although a section of the 1970 Organized Crime Act requires disclosure of any surveillance by the Attorney General to the defendant in a judicial proceeding, this provision has been violated by the Department of Justice in many cases including *Ellsberg* and *Kinoy*; the Shattuck-Friedman testimony contains many more examples. Because judges are so reluctant to question federal prosecutors' assertions and representations—although they are getting more sceptical—there doesn't seem to be much that can presently be done about the problem.

There are also indications that this secret

information may be used for improper purposes. For example, in a suit by an Arab-American named Abdeen Jabara, the FBI admitted tapping him and exchanging information about him with Zionist groups. Did this include wiretap information? And, as noted, it seems clear that in many cases, alleged "intelligence" information was actually used to get information for prosecutory purposes.

Much more could be said about national security tapping were there time and space. Its danger is obvious; small as are the protections for court-authorized taps, they are still much greater than are available with the secret and rarely reviewable national security taps. The Shattuck-Friedman testimony shows how feeble are the merely internal restraints, how poor the recordkeeping which makes it even harder to enforce the almost negligible accountability that is now feasible.

The Kissinger tap on the newsmen and governmental aides, the widespread tapping of dissidents (Martin Luther King, Jr. and other blacks) taps on dissenters and on a wide variety of Americans—all have made it clear that "national security" is often a euphemism for personal or political security in an uncomfortable echo of Charles Wilson's "What's good for GM is good for America."

The ideals, on which this country was founded and by which we still purport to live, do not allow us to countenance the kind of claim for unlimited and uncontrolled surveillance that is made in their name, whether for foreign or for domestic purposes. There are bills pending in Congress to try to exercise some control over this wild card in our constitutional deck, and hopefully, the post-Watergate climate will get them passed.

IV. THE WAR MENTALITY

The picture is thus quite clear: wiretapping is of no significant value in crime detection or crime prevention. Its primary value, both understood and intended by its proponents, is as a tool for "strategic intelligence." And even here, the results are sometimes useful, but often worthless, and at a heavy cost.

Yet much more is at stake than simply poor results and heavy expenditures. Not only is the privacy of millions of Americans invaded by these efforts to obtain "strategic intelligence," but the national attitude toward the social problems that create the dangers, both real and imagined, is distorted and corrupted. "Intelligence" is a weapon of war, and the same mentality that seeks the right to wiretap and bug fellow Americans and others, urges us on to a "war on crime," to destroy the "enemy within." It is the same mentality that uses the weapons of war against political enemies, and that justifies illegality, break-ins, and perhaps even murder against "enemies," as presidential chief domestic adviser John Ehrlichman's testimony before the U.S. Senate Watergate Committee shows. For after all, all's fair in love and war. In hearings before Senator Long's committee, one organized crime-fighter said he would do anything, regardless of legality, to fight organized crime. John Ehrlichman took a similar position with respect to the break-in on Daniel Ellsberg's psychiatrist. And, when narcotics agents terrorized innocent people in drug raids in Collinsville, Illinois, in Massachusetts, and elsewhere, that was justified in the same way—one of the top drug administrators referred to the people involved in drug activities as "vermin" and said, in effect, that everything is OK in the war against drugs. *New York Times'* columnist Tom Wicker drew appropriate parallels in his column on May 4, 1973, when he pointed out that "vermin, gooks, slopes" are all lumped together as "enemies" and subhuman. Collinsville and Cambodia, vermin and Vietnam—all are part of the same military and war-like approach to social problems.

Nor does this stop with "enemies" out there. Those with the war mentality become obsessed with informers and traitors, and surveillance takes place on those in the inner circles. The "enemies" come closer and closer. It became necessary for the Nixon Administration to bug and tap not only radicals and crooks but its own people, including William Safire, the President's speechwriter, who wrote, "in restrained fury," about being tapped. About this tapping he wrote:

'National security,' my eye—during the 37 days in July and August of 1969 that some agent in earphones was illegally (as the Supreme Court later found) listening in to my every word, I was writing the (sh!) President's message and speech on welfare reform.[34]

And the Watergate hearings disclose further that the President and his top aides were secretly taping their conversations with others and with each other.

It is this frame of mind that seeks to legitimate wiretapping, that talks of "fighting fire with fire," and of winning the war against crime. In this respect, the foreign and domestic uses run together. Prof. David Brion Davis has shown how ready Americans have been to imagine terrifying threats from conspiracies and subversion, and how the reaction has usually been excessive. In a recent review of Dumas Malone's fifth volume on Jefferson, writer Garry Wills noted how a fear of internal enemies who would undermine and destroy the foundations of the Republic, corrupted even so free a spirit as Jefferson in the Burr trial, and how such attitudes led to the notions of "un-Americanism" and the virtual outlawry of what that is supposed to cover.[35] The fears that have fed such overreactions have also produced the mentality that recognizes no restraints, that revels in "dirty tricks," and that virtually equates national with personal or political security.

Some of the dangers of such an attitude were discussed almost 40 years ago by Dr. Max Radin, the late noted law educator.

We are invited periodically, in the newspapers, from the pulpit, on the air, to engage in a war on crime. The military metaphor is so persistent and carried out in such detail, that we can scarcely help taking it for granted that somewhere before us, there is an entrenched and hostile force consisting of men we call criminals, whose purpose it is to attack Society, that is to say, us. The matter is presented as a simple enough affair, and it is assumed that if we fight valiantly, we will win and conquer the enemy.
And then? Unfortunately, we are not quite clear what is to happen then.

Last year Dean Francis A. Allen of the University of Michigan Law School wrote:

Wars are attended by certain inconveniences, and one of these is a war psychology which, with only slight encouragement from circumstances or special

pleading, can be quickly converted into a war psychosis. A society in such a mental state is not likely to achieve an accurate grasp of reality, to establish sensible priorities, or to make correct calculations of social costs involved in policy alternatives. Evidences of these distorted perceptions abound in contemporary statements about law enforcement. Thus one frequently encounters the reflex of politicians and law enforcement spokesmen that attributes disturbing criminal occurrences to nation-wide conspiracies (usually of a radical cast) or to the efforts of 'outside agitators.' Few of these assertions are ever confirmed by competent evidence.

The issue, of course, goes beyond the matter of law enforcement efficiency. One who elects to launch a war on crime should be aware that he is electing to engage in civil war.[36]

And Professor Leslie T. Wilkins has noted that the result of such thinking is evasion of the real problems by personifying them, by thinking that by catching some criminals—and these can never be more than a small percentage of law-breakers—we have contributed to a significant reduction in a crime.

All these dangers will be compounded by new technology, as surveillance devices, developed for the CIA and others for use in Vietnam against foreign enemies, are transferred to civilian life in the battle against domestic enemies.

In this nation, we have a history of fear of conspiracy, of foreign influences, a fear that has frequently produced great repression for little cause. Wiretapping is an essential element of this repression; it seeks to reach into the mind and thoughts of "the enemy within." It has little or no place in a free society and luckily there is no great need for it.

V. SOME PROPOSALS

Outright repeal of the legislation legitimating electronic surveillance is the only sensible approach. However, if that is not politically feasible, the following amendments may do some little good:

1. Ban state wiretapping. The results are very

meager; the abuses, such as judge-shopping and lengthy surveillance, are very great; and there is little basis for allowing it to continue. If allowed at all, limit the authority to tap to murder and kidnapping, carefully and properly defined.

2. The federal authority should be limited to murder, kidnapping and espionage. Congress should insist that wiretapping and bugging are not routine investigative techniques to be used for gambling and drug cases, but are dangerous devices that can be allowed only for the gravest of threats.

3. Lengthy, continuous surveillance should not be permitted. Extensions should not be granted except in rare cases. There should be a maximum of five days for any surveillance unless it is absolutely clear to a court that one additional five-day extension is necessary. Moreover, the type of conversation to be intercepted should be specifically described: the parties thereto, the subject matter, the time when it will take place. The practice of listening in on hundreds of conversations in order to catch a few that are "incriminating" must end. If it cannot, then electronic surveillance is so clearly incompatible with the Fourth Amendment that it should be prohibited entirely.

4. Room or house bugging should be prohibited. A significant number of surveillances (five percent in 1972) are of this variety, and it is especially indiscriminate. One can perhaps refrain from using a telephone, but with a room bug in the home or office, there is truly no place to be free from the "big ear." The draftsmen of the statute ignored this difference between tapping a telephone and bugging a room or a house, and ran them together, probably quite deliberately.

5. Notice must be made available to *all* people who are identifiable as having been over-heard.

6. Challenging a tap or bug should be available to anyone against whom evidence obtained from the surveillance is to be used, either directly or indirectly.

7. Damages should be available against the government for improperly authorized surveillance, except where the eavesdropper acted on his own.

8. A Study Commission has been established pursuant to the Act. It should not contain any members appointed by the Executive Branch, since it is that Branch whose acts are being evaluated. Eight members should be appointed by the majority party leaders in the House and Senate and six by the minority party leaders, with a Chairman to be chosen by the Chief Justice.

9. A joint congressional committee should be established to oversee all national security surveillance. It should obtain a detailed annual report from all agencies of the Executive Branch engaging in such surveillance and should issue a public report of the non-classified material. If national security intelligence surveillance is to be permitted, it should only be pursuant to a court order, and should be very narrowly confined.

Wiretapping and bugging are "dirty business" and it is now clear that they do not help to solve or even prevent much crime. They are expensive, time-consuming, and gravely threaten a free society. The Act should be repealed, and we should return to the flat ban of former §605, with some strengthening of the provisions for damages and other enforcement devices against such practices. If that is not politically feasible, then we should try to impose some limits on these pernicious practices that would at least bring them within hailing distance of the Bill of Rights. Perhaps the Watergate disclosures and their fallout will awaken the nation to the grave dangers it faces from "men of zeal," who often are not "well-intentioned," and are certainly "without understanding."[37]

———————

Notes to REFLECTIONS ON SIX YEARS OF
LEGITIMATED ELECTRONIC SURVEILLANCE
by Herman Schwartz

1. *New York Times*, February 2, 1974.
2. *New York Times*, May 9, 1974, p. 43, col. 7.
3. *Olmstead v. United States*, 277 U.S. 438 (1927).
4. Informal authority to gather intelligence against Fascist and Communist threats was first given to J. Edgar Hoover by President Franklin D. Roosevelt in 1936. See John Elliff, *Crime, Dissent and the Attorney General*, 154 (1971).
5. The story is told vividly and thoroughly in Victor Navasky's *Kennedy Justice* (1971) and the next few paragraphs draw on that.
6. *Kennedy Justice*, p. 49.
7. Hearings on Controlling Crime through More Effective Law Enforcement Before the Subcommittee on Criminal Laws and Procedures of the Senate Judiciary Committee, 90th Cong., 1st Sess., 957-58 (1957).
8. *Kennedy Justice*, p. 78.
9. See President's Commission on Law Enforcement and Administration of Justice, *Task Force: Organized Crime*, p. 29 (1967).
10. Hearings on Invasions of Privacy Before the Subcommittee on Administrative Practices and Procedures of the Senate Judiciary Committee, 89th Cong., 2d Sess., 1252-53. (1966).
11. *Id.* at 1954.
12. *Berger v. New York*, 388 U.S. 41 (1967); *Katz v. United States*, 389 U.S. 347 (1967).
13. 18 U.S.C. §2500 ff.
14. 18 U.S.C. §2518(1) (f).
15. 18 U.S.C. §2516(1), (2).
16. A rather elaborate analysis of the statistics and related material for 1968-71, some of which is summarized here, appears in my ACLU *Report, The Costs and Benefits of Electronic Surveillance* (1973).
17. *United States v. King*, 335 F. Supp. 523, 542-43 (S.D. Cal. 1971).
18. Elliff, *op. cit.*, p. 68.
19. *United States v. Whitaker*, 343 F. Supp. 358 (E.D. Pa. 1972), *rev'd*, 474 F. 2d 1246, (3d Cir. 1973).
20. *Buffalo Evening News*, May 21, 1974, P. 17, col. 2.
21. Edith Lapidus, *Eavesdropping on Trial*, 161 (1974).
22. *Id.* at 68.
23. There are almost no reports for the 1968 installations.
24. *Id.* at 162.
25. See 118 Cong. Rec. S11159 (daily ed. July 24, 1972). The correspondence is examined in detail in my 1973 ACLU *Report* at 84-85.
26. The cases are discussed in H. Schwartz, *The Legitimation of Electronic Eavesdropping: The Politics of "Law and Order,"* 67 Mich. L. Rev. 455, 464 (1969).
27. *United States v. White*, 401 U.S. 745 (1971).
28. Fred Graham, *The Due Process Revolution*, 273 (1970).
29. This includes the Ellsberg, Harrisburg, Leslie Bacon, Detroit Weathermen, Jewish Defense League and Chicago Conspiracy cases, and many other cases. The list is collected in the Shattuck-Friedman testimony cited earlier.
30. *Berger v. New York*, 388 U.S. 41, 55-56 (1967).
31. *Almeida-Sanchez v. United States*, 93 S. Ct. 2535 (1973); *Cady v. Dombrowski*, 93 S. Ct. 2523 (1973); *United States v. Robinson*, 94 S. Ct. 467 (1973); *Adams v. Williams*, 407 U.S. 143 (1972).
32. *Zweibon v. Mitchell*, 363 F. Supp. 936 (D.D.C. 1973), appeal pending.
33. This and the Justice Department testimony appeared in Hearings on Warrantless Wiretapping Before the Senate Subcommittee on Administrative Practices and Procedures of the Senate Judiciary Committee, 92 Cong., 2d Sess., 53 (Clark), 18 (Justice) (1972).
34. *New York Times*, August 9, 1973.
35. Garry Wills, *An Un-American Politician*, New York Review of Books, May 16, 1974, pp. 9, 11-12.
36. Allen, *Reflections on the Trials of Our Time* (Holmes Lecture 3/15/73). The Radin quote is from Dean Allen's Lecture.
37. The quoted words are from Brandeis' well-known warning in his *Olmstead* dissent about "men of zeal, well-meaning but without understanding." 277 U.S. at 479.

POLITICAL INTELLIGENCE:
CAMERAS, INFORMERS AND FILES

by Frank J. Donner, Esq.
Director, American Civil Liberties Union
Project on Political Surveillance
Yale Law School

At the outset we need to define the relationship of the subject in hand, political surveillance, with the larger conference theme—the right to privacy. We are exploring the acceptable scope of government intervention, open or clandestine, in the personal lives of individuals and the activities of associations, to be used not primarily for law enforcement purposes but for political purposes, with techniques traditionally associated with the criminal investigative process. The practices specifically pinpointed here are photography and informer infiltration directed against political activities. These and related government practices obviously threaten the privacy of their targets but this conclusion only scratches the surface.

To begin with, it is misleading to assimilate the surveillance of political activities into conventional criminal investigation. It is not only that political surveillance has travelled a historical journey separate from that of criminal investigation

but its intensity, penetration and scope are much greater. Law enforcement and crime prevention necessarily require investigations of suspects. Few would claim that such a probe constitutes an intolerable invasion of privacy. But when the state undertakes an investigation into political beliefs, expression and association, it crosses over into a wholly different area. The search for actual or potential enemies of the government necessarily embraces enormous masses of people and a huge area of their private lives—far more extensive than formal political associations and expressions. In order to make a judgment about a subject's politics, an investigator may find it necessary to probe his habits, visitors, sex life, reading preferences, use of leisure time, views on topics of the day, life-style, his educational background, the books in his library, the identity of his correspondents—the list is not a short one. Moreover, both the population of subjects and the scope of the invasion of privacy are expanded by the investigator's occupational bias, invariably negative. Why take chances when the safety of the government is at stake? And ironically, this exaggerated thinking is virtually required or "built-in," as it were, in a democratic system where only very great danger, emergency or threat can justify such extraordinary intrusion.

It is not merely that political surveillance challenges the protected freedoms of expression, as courts are beginning to recognize; it destroys the pre-condition, the matrix, for the exercise of such freedoms by inspiring widespread fear and distrust. Political surveillance—in contrast to other kinds of privacy invasions—is typically *hostile* rather than neutral or benign. And it is this hostility which tends (and here, too, in contrast to other privacy invasions) to transform surveillance, especially of unpopular minorities, from a means or instrumentality to an end in itself. The process by which the means becomes the end is facilitated by the uniquely-personalized "confrontationist" quality of political surveillance. Because it is so broad in coverage, penetrative, personal and hostile, its impact far exceeds its literal reach and results in pervasive self-censorship. Political surveillance thus produces the greatest return of repression for the least investment of power.

Conventional privacy invasions are alienating and dehumanizing, but still leave the individual with a means of altering the governmental decisions and policies which have victimized him. Political surveillance tampers with the very process by which political change is brought about. And the very gravity of its impact leads to an exaggeration of the threat which is said to justify it. Thus, the impropriety of surveillance practices is frequently masked by an invented or deceptive justification. And this same response often dominates the police agencies' claims of jurisdiction to engage in surveillance at all. Thus an operational mode of secrecy and deception is employed to evade or overcome legal constitutional and political challenges.

Over the past decade, we have seen an extraordinary burgeoning of political surveillance practices, both covert and overt. These activities are not exclusively confined to institutions on any particular governmental level but are associated with federal, state or urban agencies. The enormous increase in surveillance is best explained as a dominant response to the proliferating protest movements of the sixties—from opposition to the Vietnam War to demands for civil rights, from the youth revolt to the New Left. The fact that some of these movements for change appear to have crested hardly diminishes the need to examine the nature of this response: the history of political surveillance makes it disturbingly clear that the techniques for monitoring the dissenters became institutionalized and survive the original unrest which spawned them. A survey of the program of containment and repression of social movements of the sixties leaves little doubt of the emergence of a pattern that may well serve as a model for governmental action in a perhaps more intensified form at a future time of social failure. We need to understand it, to recognize its dangers and to curb its excesses. We can profitably focus on two outstanding surveillance "growth areas": the emergence on an urban level of photography as a weapon against protest and the normalization of informing as a counter to political dissent, a practice identified with the Federal Bureau of Investigation (FBI).

Photography and informing are not discrete phenomena unrelated to each other. They are part of a body of techniques for collecting information about a "subject," the whole of which is usually referred to as intelligence and which also includes physical surveillance, electronic eavesdropping, interrogation of "established sources"—from college deans to landlords, from bank managers to credit agencies, as well as more casual sources such as cab drivers, bartenders, teachers, parents and children. These and related practices, as well as their product—files and dossiers—can form a coherent intelligence system in which each mode of collection supplements or complements or, if necessary, substitutes for the other. Intelligence is frequently a covert art, relying heavily on secrecy and deception; but as we shall see, it has an overt side as well, typically favored when the purpose is to be aggressive and intimidating and not merely the tacit collection of data.

The functional coherence just referred to is matched by a structural interrelationship. For many years intelligence institutions on all governmental levels operated in a jurisdictional hodgepodge with gaps, overlapping, duplication and conflict. Ironically, this crazy-quilt format obscured or aborted the repressive potential of a coordinated national political police capability. Local and national intelligence agencies are beginning to coalesce into an "intelligence community." For example, the young demonstrators who came to Chicago in 1968 encountered "Red squad" operators from their home towns. These urban agents cooperated with their federal counterparts, as well as with the Army and Navy secret operatives at the Chicago demonstrations.

The flowering of this collaboration is clearly visible in the FBI's "counterintelligence" programs. COINTELPRO, which began in the late sixties and terminated in 1971. These programs (seven altogether) of disruption and demoralization of political targets were frequently implemented by urban police units through tactics such as raids and arrests on pretext for harassment purposes. The Bureau helped coordinate these tactics and furnished assistance in a variety of other ways.

Before turning to our subject areas, photography and informer infiltration, we should examine more closely the developments which have fueled this extraordinary surveillance explosion in our time. The political upheavals of the sixties gave rise on the one hand to new political initiatives and on the other to demonstrations and rallies for immediate changes and reforms, especially directed at the Vietnam War. The chosen instrument for dealing with the former was infiltration and with the latter police control and surveillance, dominated by photography. The classic justification for infiltration is a threat to the national security and, for photography, preservation of the public order. But, in both cases, the means used overshadowed the claimed justification.

The political ferment of the sixties made intelligence agencies and police units painfully aware of the inadequacy of their techniques, the limitations of their coverage and the uselessness of their files, choked with millions of dossiers of aging or dead radicals. There was an almost inevitable over-reaction and a swift embrace of new technology of identification and surveillance. New gadgetry in virtually all fields gave intelligence capabilities undreamed of by the most zealous practitioners of the repressive arts of the nineteenth century.

A third stimulus to intelligence growth claims our attention. As Watergate has made all too clear, intelligence in our time has become a mode of governance, a way of exercising governmental power which outruns the forms of law. In part, this use of official power to bypass established institutions was stimulated by the Vietnam War and it created not only a broader awareness of the efficiency of intelligence both passive and active as a means of neutralizing or overcoming an enemy, but also trained cadres in the use of these practices. In fact, every war since the Civil War has exerted similar dual influences. Beyond this, we cannot ignore the extent to which our culture has, especially in recent years, glamorized intelligence as the key to freedom and power. With the help of the media we have built a fantasy system which uses spying and spies to project longings for heroic action, for mystification —codes, passwords, disguises, deception, for the sense of power which flows from the secret knowledge of the personal lives of others and the cognate feeling of invulnerability, produced by the gadgetry of surveillance from secret transmitters to miniaturized camers. As Patrick J. McGarvey has written in *CIA – The Myth and the Madness*:

> . . . Intelligence seems to be a virility symbol for many Americans—one that immediately equates the profession with such allegedly masculine ventures as murder, coup-plotting, intrigue, and a dash of illicit love making. Their minds somehow entangle the violence of pro football, the screen antics of James Bond, and lingering World War II memories of parachuting behind enemy lines with an exaggerated sense of 'duty, honor, country'.

This same fantasy system, which glorifies the spy, paints his antagonist as bestial and inhuman. He is not merely an enemy; he is the "other," the image by which we negatively define ourselves. This antagonist is almost supernaturally crafty and seems to win every round only to be foiled at the very end by the courage and resourcefulness of the spy-hero. We have become all to familiar with this scenario through the cinema, TV and the comics. But how different from these gilded spies are their real life counterparts: the Liddys and Hunts, the Caulfields and Ulasewiczes, the Segrettis and the McCords.

Photography

The emergence of photography as a surveillance tool of urban "Red squads" dates from the early sixties. Prior to that time, physical surveillance of political and protest meetings and rallies both indoors and outdoors was not uncommon. The role of the police was generally confined to collecting literature, taking notes on speeches or checking license plate numbers to identify participants. Photography was quite rare. The monitoring personnel became quite familiar to all; the entire operation was based on a sort of bureaucratic inertia. But with the eruption of ghetto unrest, peace protests and campus activism, the picture changed.

The transformation of the intelligence role of the municipal police must be viewed in a context of mounting friction between local enforcement authorities and dissident groups. To the policeman, public protest is an unwelcome disruption of a tranquility which he regards as natural and proper. Moreover, his response to anit-war activities is particularly hostile because he sees himself as a beleaguered defender of "patriotic" values. When, as in the case of opposition to the war, protest becomes highly widespread and activist, he tends to use his power and authority aggressively to protect his threatened values. In the same way, the life-style nonconformity of youth provokes his resentment and hostility.

The changing surveillance role of the police was flavorfully described by Inspector Harry Fox of the Philadelphia police in Senate testimony a few years ago.

Police have now become 'watchdogs' and 'observers' of vocal, subversive and revolutionary minded people.

This function has been institutionalized in Philadephia in a:

civil disobedience unit composed of selected and highly trained plainclothesmen. They cover all meetings, rallies, lectures, marches, sit-ins, lay-downs, fasts, vigils or any other type of demonstration that has ominous overtones ... These officers know by sight the hard core men and women who lead and inspire demonstrations. They know their associates, family ties, techniques, and affiliations with organizations leaning toward Communism both on and off the Attorney General's list. They see them day in and day out recruiting, planning, carrying signs, and

verbally assaulting the principles of our democracy.

Yes, the police role has become one of ... surveillance, taking photographs, identifying participants, and making records of the events. On this basis, local police are able to piece together this jigsaw puzzle and see the widespread activity of the hard core demonstrators and instigators.

The role of the policeman as an adversary of dissenters leads him into right-wing politics. His professionalism is in turn undermined by his political values. And as this process develops, the policeman is increasingly tempted to resort to self-help—harassment and the tactics of guerilla warfare. His targets—activists, demonstrators and ordinary folk—are quick to sense this personal quality, frequently so dominant in the policeman's behavior; if, by his conduct, he challenges them and their cause, they feel forced either to respond in kind or to abandon their protest altogether.

In this conflict between the police and the demonstrators the camera plays an important role. Police agents in communities throughout the country systematically photograph demonstrations, parades, confrontations, vigils, rallies, presentation of petitions to Congressmen and Senators and related activities. The photographers attached to the Philadelphia Intelligence Unit covered more than one thousand demonstrations a year. Any "incident" considered "controversial" is a predictable subject for the police photographer. Activities in opposition to the Vietnam War were automatically considered "controversial" but not those in favor. In the South integrationist racial protest was accorded top photographic priority.

The group photographed may number in the thousands or not exceed three. The camera photographs the entire group as well as individual members. One may involuntarily sit for his portrait any number of times. (A friend claims to have had her picture taken over one hundred times by the police of an upstate New York city). Photographs are taken from as close as three to five feet. Police photographers sometimes openly laugh at and ridicule the demonstrators. Children who accompany their parents are photographed as are casual bystanders and non-participants. Panel trucks are sometimes used to convey and conceal photographic equipment. On occasion they are camouflaged as media vehicles (referred to by veteran surveillance subjects as "WFBI"). Surveillance photographers acquire spurious press credentials; bona fide media cameramen moonlight as police or FBI informers. Supplementary photographic data is sometimes obtained from cooperating newspapers and television stations.

Photographs are covertly taken by unobtrusive plainclothesmen when a "respectable" group is involved—for example, parents picketing a school. However, usually police personnel (on occasion in uniform) do not bother to conceal their activities. They either man the cameras themselves or give directions to aides by pointing to particular individuals or groups to be photographed. If the size or density of the crowd makes this personalized procedure impractical, photographs are taken from the closest possible location and with a lens setting permitting subsequent identification of individual participants. Photographic helicopter sweeps—a refinement in big-city intelligence practice—are ideal for very large crowds.

(The extraordinary importance of photography in the new intelligence scene was amusingly demonstrated during the Chicago conspiracy trial. By court order, to safeguard the integrity of the judicial process, photographers were excluded from the Federal Courthouse during the trial. But this prohibition unwittingly closed a valuable surveillance channel and the order was amended to permit intelligence photographers to continue to ply their trade.)

Photography has (and is intended to have) an intimidating effect on the subject. Most police functionaries will privately admit this, although their public justifications for the practice are quite decorous and reassuring. These range from a claimed need to have a record "in case there is a disturbance" to the value of photographs as an instructional tool in lectures to policemen on "crowd control." The true purpose is frequently exposed when it turns out that the police cameramen have been pretending to snap pictures long after they have run out of film. When asked about this, a member of an anti-subversive unit explained, "Sometimes I go out on an assignment with an empty camera. Just taking the pictures cools the agitators."

What has been said up to now about the application and scope of photographic surveillance is quite misleading because it omits the impact of technology. In contrast to other fields the new developments in photographic technology and the related fields of optics and electronics have already had a measurable impact. Even as photography was emerging as a surveillance tool, it underwent rapid technological changes which: (1) expanded the coverage area; (2) lengthened the possible distance between the subject and the police camera; (3) made twenty-four hour surveillance feasible; (4) concealed both the identity of the cameraman and even the fact that the picture was being taken; and (5) made possible instantaneous review and identification. Technology has not only vastly improved the efficiency of photography as a surveillance tool, but it has perfected its covert capability. Of course, these advances are supposed to serve law enforcement purposes, but it would be folly to ignore their impact not only on privacy generally, but on freedom of political expression in particular.

Still photography remains the foundation stone of police camera work. During demonstrations, the members of the anti-subversive squads and their auxiliaries are readily identifiable by their Pentaxes. A more sophisticated instrument combines high powered binoculars, a camera and a telecamera. This device enables the policeman to stand more than half a mile away and take clear identifiable pictures of an area as large as a football field. Another camera, the Cyclops, permits surveillance at night. The Cyclops is an electro-optical device which converts light to electricity. It permits photography both at night and in the daytime. The luminance gain is extaordinarily high; the night vision scope is quite undetectable because it gives off no light. The range is determined only by terrain and the size of the objective to be viewed.

But it is television and videotape which have truly revolutionized photographic surveillance. The application of low-light-level television (LLLTV) to cable systems permits videotaping at night. The system does not radiate a beam as infrared systems do and, therefore, is impossible to detect when in use. Through this system an area is viewed and everything the camera sees is recorded on videotape, while at the same time the images are projected on a screen. Its police applications are almost limitless.

The use of television coupled with helicopters for crowd viewing is also spreading. In Washington, D.C. the Police Department uses television cameras to survey demonstrations and crimes. The television camera can be installed in any of the Department's three helicopters and monitored at the Police Operations Center where, in addition, two-way radio communication is maintained with the helicopters, squad cars and patrolmen. The videotape recordings are retained in police files as evidence. In addition, the surveillance capability includes portable television cameras which, according to a police official, "look just like a commercial T.V. camera" and can be carried by a plainclothes officer for close-in surveillance of crowds.

Universities are acquiring this surveillance equipment at a rapid rate. They are becoming "pilot" areas in which surveillance takes place on a comprehensive scale. With the aid of LEAA funds, a Cleveland, Ohio educational and cultural community known as University Circle has served as a test area for a highly sophisticated surveillance system. Everyone walking the streets within a two square mile area can be viewed by at least one of the two television cameras installed on the top of two high buildings. The image taken by the cameras is transmitted to police headquarters by laser beam. Theoretically, a single beam can carry over one million television signals simultaneously. The cameras tilt, pan, scan and zoom, and are so powerful that an operator on the first floor of the police station can count the number of stones in the wall of a church one-half mile away (see *Cleveland Plain Dealer*, July 28, 1972).

Street surveillance by closed circuit television cameras has become commonplace. These systems operate in cities such as San Francisco, Mount Vernon, Hoboken, New Jersey and New York City. They usually consist of stationary low-light-level television cameras positioned on the top of buildings or on high poles and supplemented by similar cameras capable of tilting, panning and zooming. All of the cameras are usually encased in what is known as "environmental housing" and protected from rain by windshield wipers. They are designed to function in temperatures from -20°F to 140° and can be remotely controlled to tilt, pan, zoom and rotate 355 degrees. Such equipment permits the police to obtain the close-up of faces a half mile away even in darkness.

Probably the most sophisticated system of all is New York City's "War Room" system established in 1969, as described in an article in the *New York Times*:

> The system comprises a TV camera, zoom lens, image stabilizer, and microwave transmitting equipment installed in a helicopter. The signal is received at the Empire State Building via antennae. The signal is then relayed via microwave television links to Police Headquarters. The signal can be distributed to various offices throughout the building, including the Command and Control Center, where the information can be evaluated and manpower and equipment assigned to cope with the problem. The installation is equipped with recording equipment so that a permanent record can be made of the transmitted audio and visual signals. Live television images can also be projected on a six-foot by eight-foot screen for close observation.

> Receiving antennae on the Empire State Building provide 360 degrees of coverage to enable the helicopter to fly in any direction and still transmit back to the Empire State Building. The helicopter's omnidirectional antenna provides flight flexibility as well.

It will be only a matter of time before sophisticated photographic equipment, based upon the LLLTV cabled or uncabled television, and lasers become standard operational equipment. Today almost every reasonably well-equipped police agency boasts sophisticated photographic equipment as well as training facilities. In some cases photographic specialists are sent for special training and on their return instruct others. The psychological deterrence of this new photographic weaponry (there is no other word for it) has yet to be measured. But who can doubt that it presents a formidable hazard to freedom of expression and association.

Informer Infiltration

If photography is the surveillance trademark of the urban "Red squads", the infiltration of the informers is the favorite surveillance instrumentality of the Federal Bureau of Investigation. All surveillance agencies on every level of government use political informers but the Bureau's use of informers is far more pervasive. Informer infiltration is the classic response to political protest and dissidence. Again, the invasion of privacy it involves is overshadowed by its impact on First Amendment freedoms. Informers have always served to curb minorities and bolster despotic rule. They have been used against the Jews and Christians in Roman times, non-Catholics under the Medieval Inquisition, Catholics in seventeenth century England, Colonists in eighteenth century America, slaves seeking emancipation in the nineteenth century, British reformers in the England of Pitt and Castlereagh, the British Chartist and Trade Union movement of the nineteenth century, the Continental Socialist and Communist movements of the same era, the struggle for Irish independence, the labor movement in America from its very beginning, and all of American radical movements from the First World War until the present.

Political informers in the service of the FBI fall into three classes: the "plant," who is recruited for the express purpose of infiltrating a target group; the informer who is already "in place," i.e. a bona fide member of a group who is induced to spy on it; and the defector or renegade. The plant is the most common kind of informer. As a former agent said in an interview:

> Your best bet ... was to get somebody who was completely unconnected with the organization, preferably somebody on the college campus, some kid who was young enough to fit in the group, had time to spare and was willing to cooperate and then put him in the group cold ... It was rare you got an informant who was already established in an organization because first of all you couldn't talk to him without getting the door slammed in your face ... so you usually tried to recruit somebody fresh and new.

The planted infiltrator is a more valuable tool than the defector, who leaves the group because of an ideological quarrel or some other difference. The defector can supply information about the group's size, composition and leadership but he cannot serve as a source of continuing information. He "co-operates with the FBI" (a classic euphemism) first through a process of debriefing and then as a witness. But even as a witness the defector has questionable value. His bias and eagerness for revenge frequently break through his recitals on the witness stand. From the Bureau's point of view, the plant has another advantage over the defector on the witness stand. It is easier to claim that he was motivated purely by patriotism and is untainted by prior subversion, by guilt, revenge or self-justification.

But whether "in place," a "plant," a lapsed member induced to return or a defector, the informer is the classic instrument of political intelligence and remains indispensable despite the growing resort to electronic surveillance. In fact, the Warren Court's limitations on the scope of wire-tapping and bugging have themselves led to a heavier reliance on informing as a substitute. Moreover, these limitations have encouraged the use of informers because they can supply "probable cause" of a crime and so justify a judicial order permitting wiretapping.

Even when curbs on electronic surveillance are ignored or circumvented, informers are a superior vehicle for political espionage. Electronic eavesdropping and wiretapping are haphazard and limited forms of surveillance, ill-suited to the slow pace, ambiguity, confusion and factionalism of the dissenting political activities that are targets of intelligence. Moreover, wiretaps can be neutralized once the subject becomes aware of them, or—as is more frequently the case—suspects their use.

Nor are informers displaced by cameras or tape recorders. As photography has increased in importance as a surveillance tool, the recruitment of informer-photographers has intensified. They are paid a bonus, especially if they are in a position to furnish photos otherwise unattainable by the agent. For example, Louis Salzberg, a New York photographer, received about $10,000 in the two years he served as an FBI informer. He used this money to finance a studio which sold pictures to leftist publications, the negatives of which were turned over to the FBI. He surfaced at the Chicago conspiracy trial and subsequently testified before the House Internal Security Committee, which was also supplied with negatives as well as the documents and correspondence taken by Salzberg from the files of the Veterans for Peace and the Fifth Avenue Peace Parade Committee.

The procedures for developing informers are by now routine. The informant is first used and is paid for specific items of information. At this stage he is known as a "PSI" (potential security informant) or "PRI" (potential racial informant). After he is "developed" by the agent and proves his worth, he becomes an "SI" or "RI" and is described as a "reliable informant" or "an informant of known reliability"—embellishments derived from legal requirements. The informer then acquires a file, a code symbol and a name or initials, this last for the purpose of security inside the Bureau. A method and place of reporting is agreed upon and supplementary channels of communication are established. He is usually paid a fixed stipend which he might begin receiving even as a PSI and which is increased from time to time as his usefulness grows. While some informers agree to serve for patriotic reasons, the dominant motivation for informing is money. As of about two years ago the going rate was $400 a month, plus substantially-paid expenses and bounty payments.

As it was with Judas, so it remains today. Napoleon greatly valued his spy, Schulmeister, and said of him that one spy in the right place is worth 20,000 men in the field. But when it came time to reward this extraordinary man for his services, Napoleon refused him the Legion of Honor for which he had been recommended and commented that money was the only suitable reward for a spy.

Even when other reasons (patriotism, an arrested adolescence, revenge) inspire the spy initially to enter into the relationship, the cash becomes the *raison d'etre*. The would-be patriot who begins by spurning payment as a rebuke to his ideals, usually ends by accepting money and, indeed, becoming dependent on his informer earnings as a supplement to his income. In an interview, a recanted FBI student informer told me, "When I first went to work for the Bureau, I thought it would be a lark; besides, I would be defending my country. As I became involved, I rose in the (Communist) Party to a position of leadership. My payments for services rose at the same time. I was making enough money to pay my way through school, not counting the trips to attend Party schools and conventions in various parts of the country that the FBI paid for as 'expenses.' I was really living the good life. I became a Marxist of sorts and, as I became committed, I realized how dependent I had become on the FBI."

The economic incentive is sharpened when, as is sometimes the case, the informer is paid a fixed amount for each meeting he attends or when, even though he is already on salary, he is paid a bonus for a particular item of information. Here is how an ex-agent describes these special payments: "The standard handbook rule was that you paid the informant on the basis of the value of the information received ... I had an informant who would hold me up for money every once in a while. The informant would call me on the phone and say, 'I've got something hot, what's it worth to you?' And I'd come up with a figure, 'OK, I'll give you fifty bucks for it if it's worth it,' and usually it was worth money because this particular informant was good." The agent added, "Especially in the racial field, the main consideration was money." There is no room for doubt that the entire system of undercover espionage in this country is bought and paid for by the Bureau. Without its generous payment scales and inducements, it would collapse overnight.

Political informers must be sharply distinguished from the informants—the tipsters, decoys, plants or defectors—who supply evidence of law violation. In the criminal case the infiltrator is planted only when the police agency has probable cause to believe that a crime is being planned and he operates only long enough to obtain this evidence and possibly abort a criminal scheme. The duration and depth of the informer's penetration is limited by the needs of law enforcement on the one hand and a regard for the plant's physical well-being on the other.

In contrast, the political informer enters into an on-going relationship with the Bureau and with his targets. Only a tiny fraction of the political informers devote themselves to collection of evidence for law enforcement purposes. For the most part they are engaged in on-going, open-ended surveillance—people watching. Political informing is part of the politics of deferred reckoning, a projection of the thesis that at some time in the future there will be an apocalyptic showdown with the evil forces of subversion—radicals, revolutionaries and subversives—and in preparation for this is the need to keep informed of who "they" are and what "they" are up to.

Spies help to create a public climate of fear and subversion. They also directly intimidate target groups and their members and seriously interfere with freedom of association. The subject's knowledge, suspicion or fear that his political activities are under surveillance by an informer is a serious restraint. The informer system is marvelously efficient because the relatively open character of our society is psychologically disarming and makes the average subject highly vulnerable to fear when his politics come under secret scrutiny by an arm of government, especially the FBI, which is known to identify dissent with subversion. The undercover character of the investigation, the benighted standards of the informer, the assumed guilt of the subject, the denial of an opportunity to answer any charges and confront the accuser can be shattering.

Surveillance is an especially attractive weapon in a democracy with explicit constitutional limitations on invasions of free expression because its sanctions are submerged. It is "only" an investigation of the "facts" we are told; it neither enjoins nor punishes political expression and activities. Yet it can hardly be denied that the self-censorship which it stimulates is far more damaging than many express statutory or administrative restraints.

The chilling impact of the informer has never been as expressively described as in this passage by the English constitutional historian, Sir Erskine May, written in 1866:

Next in importance to personal freedom is immunity from suspicions and jealous observation. Men may be without restraints upon their liberty; they may pass to and fro at pleasure; but if their steps are tracked by spies and informers, their words noted down for crimination, their associates watched as conspirators—who shall say that they are free? Nothing is more revolting to Englishmen that the espionage which forms part of the administrative system of continental despotisms.

It haunts men like an evil genius, chills their gayety, restrains their wit, casts a shadow over their friendships, and blights their domestic hearth. The freedom of a country may be measured by its immunity from this baleful agency. Rulers who distrust their own people must govern in a spirit of absolutism; and suspected subjects will be ever sensible of their bondage.

The Bureau's informer system has added a new dimension to the evils described by May: it has been transformed from a mere investigative means into an end in itself. The recruitment of informers is *intended* to stigmatize target groups and individuals and to restrain them or frighten them into silence. This explains why informers are kept in organizations for years, turning in worthless, tedious and repetitious reports. And why, within the same infiltrated organization, many informers may be paid for similar reports about precisely the same meetings.

In the overwhelming majority of cases, it is not the information furnished by the spy which makes him a prized Bureau asset but the fact that he is there—a presence which intimidates and demoralizes his targets. It is this coercive aim that explains the curious dualism in American infiltration practice: while the identity of the individual informer is concealed, the fact that there is a widespread network of informers in the American Left is widely publicized.

One cannot limit the case against informers to issues of privacy and repression. The informer develops his cover, dispels suspicion and obtains information through deception and betrayal.

In the Christian tradition, the informer is denounced and excoriated as a betrayer. "The talebearer shall defile his own soul, and be hated by all." Ecclesiasticus, XXXI, 31. The Bible story of Judas Iscariot powerfully projects the image of horror and revulsion which informing stirs in the Christian imagination. The informer is a universal object of loathing because he undermines the mutual trust which is an indispensable precondition of social relations. He strikes at the roots of community. Obscurely but unmistakably President Nixon summed it all up when, according to the transcript of the White House tapes, he told John Dean on February 28, 1973, "The informer is not one in our society. They say no civilized (characterization deleted) informs."

There is no way for an informer to avoid betrayal. In order to overcome suspicion he must become friendly with the target and share the social life of his victims. His wife and children must be used to further the deception. He wins trust in order to do his targets injury. Not that men are grudging of their trust. On the contrary; if feelings of persecution and of distrust are symptoms of a pathology, then trust and acceptance are healthy. We legitimize the stranger because trust is a human need. This vulnerability, this need to trust, prevails even when obvious risks require caution. The victim is shamed by his doubts because they mock his humanity, his sense of himself in relation to others. In short, the informer preys on what is best in man.

Consider the case of Mr. and Mrs. William Bond. They testified before the Subversive Activities Control Board in April 1964 that they had joined the Communist Party in 1960 as paid informers for the government. Appearing as a defense witness was their 20-year-old son. He had assumed that his parents were bona fide Communists when he had attended a meeting with them. But subsequently they took him to a conference with their Bureau contact, who asked him to become an informer like his parents. Young Bond testified that he pleaded with his parents to discontinue their association with the Bureau. He explained, "The whole question of being an informer became repugnant to me. These people were their friends. I had been taught, 'You don't tattle. You don't squeal'."

He tried unsuccessfully to convince his parents to end their relationship with the Bureau and left home after several arguments. On cross-examination, Mrs. Bond was asked: "You even informed on your son?" "Yes," she answered. When asked why she had informed on people who had befriended her, she replied, "I am an American. They were my enemies." "You wanted to expose the enemies of America?" "That is right." "You accepted these people's hospitality and offers of friendship? ... You have lived a sort of double life; you have pretended to be these people's friend?" "Yes." "Your motives were patriotic?" "Yes."

"You did this to aid your country?", the lawyer pressed the witness. "Yes ... I grew up in a land of freedom and I wanted my boys to grow up in a land of freedom," Mrs. Bond sobbed in reply. (The Bonds have four sons; William is the oldest.)

The informer system functions as a means of bribing men to betray their fellows. Here is an account from an interview with an ex-agent:

"I had an informant in the Nation of Islam, a Black Muslim group. He was sick for quite a while and sent in reports that were completely useless; but we continued to pay him. Finally he had to be hospitalized. While he was in the hospital he was visited by some of the Brothers. They left him a get well card which they all signed. He sent me the card and asked me to accept it as a substitute for a regular report and pay him his monthly reimbursement for services because he needed the money very badly."

Emerson Poe was the best friend of Scott Camil, a Florida VVAW leader. They enjoyed each other's company, and spent much time together. Camil's girl friend, Nancy McCown, visited the Poes on many occasions. When Mrs. Poe had a miscarriage, Miss McCown came over for consolation and to help with the household chores. She and Camil also visited and helped out when Poe became ill and, on one occasion, helped decorate the Poe's Christmas tree. The Poes were equally hospitable and helpful. They organized a surprise birthday party for Miss McCown at their house and invited Miss McCown's parents. On August 17, 1973, Poe appeared as a surprise witness against Camil in a federal prosecution and testified that his relationship to Camil was instigated by the FBI, that his friendship was simulated and that he had been a paid informer from the beginning.

Many targets find it difficult to accept the fact that the informer is a plant—a deceiver from the beginning—rather than a defector whose initial bona fide commitment was abandoned out of weakness, fear or external pressure. This consoling, self-protective interpretation may well be an accurate version of the inner reality. The informer is rarely a

cool role-player, untouched by his intended victims or their causes. The plant gives a great deal to the target group and its members. Some of his contributions are, of course, motivated by the need to preserve his cover.

But it is a forgery of normal inter-personal relations to suppose that an informer merely confines himself to the minimum required to disarm suspicion. To be sure, his contributions typically embrace such routine organizational chores as distributing leaflets, attending meetings, financial support and proselytizing new members. In addition, the spy frequently contributes some special skill or resource which increases his value to the group. He may be an expert chauffeur (like Gene Roberts in the Panther 21 case), a well-muscled bodyguard (like Robert Pierson in the Chicago conspiracy case), enjoy a unique degree of mobility and access to others (Boyd F. Douglas, Jr. in the Harrisburg conspiracy case), know where to buy dynamite (Raymond Wood in the Statue of Liberty case), be familiar with explosives and firearms (Tommy the Traveller, who incited Hobart campus violence), have unusual financial resources (Horace Parker in the Seattle 7 case) or know how to solve technical problems which frustrate the target (Robert Hardy and the Camden 28). These contributions, especially when brought to the aid of people for whom they are indispensable because of their powerlessness, impracticality or poverty, can spell the difference between success or failure.

Even the more passive informer typically gives more of himself (and of his energies) than the role demands. As an ex-student informer told me:

I began to like the people and to enjoy being with them. They cared about me in a way that was new to me. Besides, I learned a lot and I got turned on—at first by the program and then by the actions. When I led the campus demonstrations I did it because I wanted to. Of course, when I got home that night I wrote it up in my report. But I began to feel like a (expletive deleted).

In short, many informers betray not only their targets but themselves. And the informer is sometimes forced to confront this self-betrayal by the form in which his reports are cast. Assertedly for security purposes, the informer is required to report not only on others but on himself. "Pretend you are a light bulb in a fixture at the top of the ceiling shining down into the room. Your reports should cover everything that is said by everybody, including yourself." An informer who acted on these instructions for a number of years told me:

"At first I felt as though I was finking on myself and didn't report half the stuff I said at meetings. Then I began to realize that my whole position was untenable. I managed to live with my guilt by becoming more involved. After a while I became 90% Marxist and 10% informer. What was happening was that I was selling out in my reports at night the things that I lived for and believed in during the day."

Finally, one cannot ignore the fact that the risk of provocation is inherent in infiltration, even when it is not part of a planned intelligence strategy. The merely passive informer observer can not hope to play more than a lowly "go-fer" role in the target group if he gains entry at all. In order to enhance his usefulness he must penetrate planning circles by becoming highly active. This pressure, along with the need to preserve cover, often drives the infiltrator into provocative acts, regardless of the official cautionary advice which he may be given when he receives his assignment—a gesture routinely made for the record, as a defense against a possible charge of entrapment. When the informer comes to share the values of his victims (a not infrequent phenomenon as I have indicated), his newly-acquired convictions carry him far beyond the call of duty. His secret knowledge that he alone in the group is immune from accountability for his acts dissolves all restraint on his zeal. Infiltrators also include professional police agents who coldly engineer a single provocative act designed to "set-up" the leaders of the target group for round-up and arrest.

Files and Dossiers

The end products of intelligence are files, dossiers and indices—biographies about individuals and their organizations. The files are the working capital of intelligence, an assurance of continuity and funding even when the political climate is unfavorable. The mere fact that data appears in a file in itself becomes a warrant of its truth and accuracy, automatically raising it above the level of its source, however dubious it might otherwise be. As Stanton Wheeler has observed (in *On Record*, p. 5), "a file or dossier is likely to attain a *legitimacy* and *authority* that is lacking in more informal types of communication ... We talk about the kind of record a person develops, typically meaning the sorts of formal evaluations contained in files and dossiers."

Files contribute to the mystique of professionalism. The reduction of a mass of material into subversive classifications, of events into a chronological sequence, of names by alphabetical order, can somehow clothe a body of questionable data, assembled by the most arbitrary and unreliable standards, with a special aura of objectivity and professionalism. The serried ranks of file cabinets join the microscope, camera, and electronic transmitter as valuable instruments of scientific investigation. In short, the process by which material is organized inevitably comes to serve as a mask for its relevance or probative value.

Political files reinforce and deepen the restraining or chilling effect produced by surveillance. Their mere existence, no matter how limited their access, inspires fear. Files "document" the intelligence thesis that dissent is a form of political original sin—permanent, incurable and contagious. They impose on the political life of the individual a "record" which he cannot change; they make him a "subject," tied forever to political views and associations which he may have long since abandoned.

It is the special need to feed names into the file system which makes the informer such an important intelligence input. The informer is encouraged to give the highest priority to the identification of individuals, and not to concern himself too much with "line" or theory. As an ex-agent put it, "The great stress with your informant is on names, especially of the leadership and then, from there, report names of individuals who are a moving force in the organization, who are the committee chairmen, who are the organizers."

Here is a description by a recently resigned Bureau agent of how the informer's reports are processed for filing in individual and organization dossiers:

In D.C. we have an individual file and an organizational file ... We start out by investigating an organization; then we had compiled a big file on the organization itself, we'd start investigating all of the officers in the organization on an individual basis and then prominent members of the organization, also on an individual basis. Each one of these people would have a separate file on them and into that file would go, first of all, all the background information we could dig up on a guy—from whatever source we could get it from. Then we'd go into all of the informant's statements that identified him at a given meeting or at a given demonstration or rally. Then also would go into the reports from other agencies that this guy had done such and such.

The agent then summarized and interpreted the reports and this would mean his interpretation of everything that was said about the guy. Any subject that was going to be around or was in a prominent position, the agent would have to report on to the Bureau. And he would do this by making up a report, which was supposed to be a kind of factual report, but he would take and extrapolate from all of this mass of information he got from an informant a synopsis or a summary of all the activities the guy had been in.

Informers are encouraged to develop relationships with organizations or to obtain posts such as recording secretary which gives them access to membership lists (and are sometimes rewarded with a bonus for this feat). Many informers recruit members for the groups they infiltrate and turn in their names. Informers have, on occasion, been paid on the basis of the names they report. When the informer surfaces and appears before a congressional committee, the heart of his testimony is a detailed identification and description of his former associates. This is done not only to generate possible sanctions against the individuals thus exposed, but to fatten the committee's files as well as those of other intelligence agencies.

The indiscriminate accumulation of names is a logical expression of the intelligence dogma that individual evil men—agitators—artificially stimulate political and social unrest. If a subject does not qualify for the "security index," the "rabble-rouser" or the "agitator index," he still is entered into the files because he is a member of an organization or is present at a meeting. And, as we have seen from the Media papers, he may be singled out and named in the Bureau files even if the group in which he is active has done nothing which warrants surveillance.

Political surveillance collects intelligence information which has little practical operational value but is considered vital for long-range purposes. It is classified as "strategic" (as opposed to line) intelligence and consists of biographical files and indices. Names are strategically important because surveillance operations are premised on the politics of deferred reckoning. Such files are "warehoused"; that is, they are stored and kept current against a future time when information about the subject's background may become valuable. It is rare that a filing system involving other forms of conduct would preserve records of behavior or transactions dating back twenty or thirty years or would indiscriminately preserve data about the quick as well as the dead; but this is routine in the intelligence world. After all, a seemingly obsolete entry, a record dating back to the forties, might provide a vital clue to a subversive conspiracy. The best gauge of the political slant of a subject is the way the twig was bent long ago.

The fact that the subversives have not yet made their final move to take over is hardly proof that the past collection, filing and analysis of millions of items was unjustified. Only the vigilance of intelligence has up until now warded off the holocaust.

The files create a usable past; they extend the political scope of intelligence in still another direction. By storing personal data about varied forms of political involvement, the sheer accumulation of items—the signature on a peace petition, presence at a demonstration protesting welfare cuts, receipt of left-wing literature, a speech at a panel on police brutality—each innocuous in itself, leads the intelligence mind to the conclusion that the subject is subversive. Quantity is transformed into quality; the end result is greater than the sum of its parts.

Intelligence files are a highly important resource in the development of support for the ideology of intelligence, the institutional intelligence community and its friends. It is also an effective weapon in discrediting its critics. Urban "Red squads," for example, funnel file material to friendly officials and media representatives. The anti-subversive units in Chicago, New York and Philadelphia, for example, have all used files to help friends and to discredit critics. The New York City "Red squad"—Bureau of Special Services (BOSS)—

made this a regular practice until the late sixties. At the 1963 libel trial brought by John Henry Faulk, it was revealed that one of the defendants, Vincent Hartnett, had operated a highly profitable "smear and clear" service, in which he exposed individuals in the entertainment world and used the threat of exposure to extract investigative fees from sponsors. When Hartnett was asked on the witness stand to reveal the source of his extensive information about individuals, he testified that he had called BOSS Lieutenant Crain some seventy times for information or verification of the political background of certain entertainers and writers, and that on thirty occasions he received information from BOSS files (Faulk, *Fear on Trial,* N.Y, 1964, p. 326).

In 1970, Philadelphia's anti-subversive Police Chief, Lieutenant George Fencl, boasted to a nationwide television audience:

We have made a record of every demonstration that we handled in the city of Philadelphia and reduced this to writing, first by report and then taking out the names of persons connected with the different movements. We have some 18,000 names and we made what we call an alphabetical file. We make a 5"x8" card on each demonstrator that . . . we handle. This card shows such information as the name, address, picture if possible, and a little run down on the person . . . which group he pickets with and so forth. Also, on the back of the card we show the different demonstrations, date, time, and location and the groups that the person has picketed with. We have some 600 different organizations that we've encountered in the Philadephia area.

Frank L. Rizzo, first as Philadephia Police Commissioner—then as Mayor—used the files to silence his critics. In the course of a feud in the late sixties, he told members of the Board of Education, "I've got enough on every one of you . . . to run you out of the city." When he ran for Mayor in 1971 he boasted to the Press that he "had something on" all of his opponents in a primary election.

But far more ominous was FBI Director J. Edgar Hoover's exploitation of file material. Under his directorship, the Bureau regularly used file material to attack critics—usually by deliberate leak of file material to news media supporters. The Director also used the files to blackmail hostile legislators. According to recent verified disclosures, he even placed the Bureau's investigative resources at the disposal of legislative supporters for use against political challengers.

The authority to maintain files—both on the urban and federal levels—is clouded. The Bureau's total file collection (not confined to political subjects) consists of six and a half million files and fifty-eight million index cards, growing at the rate of nine hundred thousand a year. These cards list both primary subjects of investigation and individuals who are collaterally referred to in the files. This enormous file collection has acquired a life of its own. Recently the Bureau's authority to develop political files unrelated to law enforcement has been sharply challenged by the court's decision in the case of *Menard v. Mitchell*. The urban anti-subversive unit files are also very impressive numerically. Until the early seventies, when a reduction was ordered, BOSS alone had custody of over a million political files.

The extraordinary durability of political files is suggested by the fact that, when Attorney General Harlan F. Stone ordered the Bureau house-cleaning in 1924, he resisted appeals to purge the files on the ground that this could only be accomplished by an Act of Congress. In the same way, the Bureau has professed that it is powerless to destroy some admittedly illegal file collections without explicit authority.

Political files have had a powerful impact on the American political imagination. They are the materials of a home-made political art form, the "documented expose," a species of political polemic now identified with the Far Right. File collections and biographies of leftists and dissenters are considered a treasured resource in the fight against subversion. The U.S. House Internal Security Committee is an important channel of such materials to its right wing following. The Committee has a file collection on more than seven hundred and fifty thousand subjects, i.e. individuals about whom political data has been collected. This collection is the special concern of the Committee's "File and Reference Section." This filing operation, along with other practices such as the development of elaborate indices consisting only of names, the publication of photographs of targets, the systematic production of propaganda and the Committee's complete irrelevance to the legislative process, emphasize what has long been apparent— that the Committee (along with its U.S. Senate counterpart) is in essence an intelligence unit which uses a claimed legislative purpose as a cover in the same way that law enforcement serves as a cover for police intelligence agencies.

Some Modest Proposals

The practices here discussed are unified by their common impact on our protected freedoms. Therefore, the need to curb them has a special urgency. They share a second characteristic: they are all rooted in jurisdictional overgrowth. The authority of local and federal police agencies to engage in political surveillance unrelated to law enforcement ("intelligence-type" investigations as they are sometimes called) is highly questionable. The process whereby conventional law enforcement agencies assume the power to monitor dissent has become tiresomely familiar.

In contrast to European countries, we have never in our history authorized, on any governmental level, a political police force, i.e., a special body responsible for the safety of government, independent of all other instruments of state administration, enjoying unlimited jurisdiction and autonomy. American intelligence practices have evolved as an illegitimate offspring of law enforcement. Usurpations of power by police units have been left unchecked primarily because they became identified with vital interests. The attitude has been: Why worry about questions of authority when the survival of the government itself is at stake? In the same way on the urban level, the monitoring of dissent was derived from police responsibility for public order. Once their intelligence functions were accepted, the implementing practices (such as photography, informers and files) were justified on the simple basis of professionalism. After all, the intelligence functionary was the expert and knew how to accomplish his unit's "mission" (to use the intelligence term) better than a mere civilian concerned with civil liberties and privacy. To this exaggerated view of the intelligence mission and the claim of professionalism was fused an insistence on secrecy and autonomy. As a result, an agency of government which poses an unacceptable threat to the democratic process itself has become virtually immune from accountability and correction. A stock-taking is imperatively needed. It is not too much to say that the growth of political intelligence implicates the most basic civil liberties issues of our time.

To begin with the urban units. The intelligence functions of these units are typically not based on statute or ordinance. They are simply the creatures of internal regulation, organizational charts and operational manuals. Similarly, political file and photograph collections which have proliferated in recent years enjoy no special authorization but are simply viewed as a functional part of the intelligence operation. The long overdue surgery on urban political intelligence will not be accomplished on the initiative of the patient—although former New York Police Commissioner Patrick Murphy did make some reforms. We are dealing here with questions of abuse of power; therapy can only be achieved through the intervention of the electorate and its representatives in municipal government. The challenge here is especially demanding because, if the past is to be a guide, the local urban and state intelligence forces may well be called upon to play a dominant role in policing dissent in the years ahead.

Informer abuse, identified here with the FBI, must be seen as the fruit of a usurped jurisdiction. As has been argued in detail elsewhere, (see *Nation*, June 1, 1974), the Bureau, despite the claims of its Director J. Edgar Hoover over the years, lacks an intelligence mandate either from Congress or the Executive Branch. The claim to an ongoing intelligence jurisdiction, based on the prevention of crimes which have a political dimension, is insupportable because intelligence practices, such as infiltration, are typically undertaken wholly without relationship to law violations, long before the punative crime is incubated and in flagrant disregard of the subject's First Amendment rights. The activation of such intelligence programs adds to the damaged rights of the target the fraud of its justification.

Nor can the Presidential directive of September 6, 1939 and its progeny supply the missing jurisdictional link. These directives, as their language, context, and background plainly establish, were concerned with war-connected offenses (such as espionage and sabotage) and besides, were limited to the emergencies which produced them. If this argument is sound, authority for the Bureau's political file accumulation cannot be derived from an intelligence-gathering mandate. Nor, as the legislative history shows, can filing authority be predicated on independent legislation, confined as it is to the law enforcement field.

Surveillance of political activities in a democracy should be confined to law enforcement, as it was in the period from 1901 to 1909, without, be it added, a measurable impact on our freedom. To the perennial complaint that new threats to our security have emerged beyond the reach of law enforcement, one must only reply that such claims have been historically overstated and are premised on the false notion that perfect security is a feasible goal for a modern society. The pursuit of such a goal leads directly to a police state.

If we do need legislation to purge the Bureau's files of data already illegally accumulated, such a measure claims a high legislative priority, especially in view of President Nixon's concern for the privacy of our people. And, whatever the fate of the House Internal Security Committee is to be, its accumulation and distribution of political files and photographs are indefensible. They serve no legitimate purpose, flout freedom of expression and association and invade privacy. A simple act of a majority of the House is all that is required to eliminate this repressive relic of the past.

The foregoing proposals attack the power to conduct political investigations unrelated to law enforcement and are based solely on the contention that intelligence is a usurped jurisdiction. While a legislative act would be the most efficient way of curtailing intelligence, it is not the only way. Litigation is also a promising route. Lawyers must begin to demythify intelligence and examine more critically its claims to legitimacy. Legislators also have a special "mission"; to undertake an objective probe of the problem of security and its relationship to political freedom. If such an examination determines that there is a genuine need for political data collection in a limited area (such as foreign intelligence), the activation of such a program and its continuing supervision should be a Congressional and not Executive responsibility, as Associate Justice William O. Douglas has recently urged.

Even if police agencies are deprived of intelligence jurisdiction, at least two problems would continue to plague us. (1) Past experience has demonstrated that law enforcement is used as a cover for political intelligence and it would be realistic to assume that, as current FBI pronouncements already indicate, the old practices would continue under a new rubric—the prevention of crimes with a political cast. And (2), the elimination of political surveillance would still leave unremedied informer abuses in the field of conventional criminal investigation. Operational controls are necessary as an alternative or as a supplement to jurisdictional curbs. The most important of these is an outright ban on the use of infiltrators and informers who are agents of the government in all cases which substantially implicate the First Amendment, whether or not a statutory violation is involved. The scope and character of the quarantined area would of course be defined with as great precision as possible and, in addition, would be made a responsibility of the Attorney General. The sanctions for violation could be adapted from the wiretap statute. This proposal has a compelling constitutional justification. In *United States v. United States District Court*, Mr. Justice Powell explained why:

Though physical entry of the home is the chief evil against which the wording of the Fourth Amendment is directed, its broader spirit now shields private speech from unreasonable surveillance ... Fourth Amendment protections become the more necessary when the targets of official surveillance may be those suspected of unorthodoxy in their political beliefs ... The price of lawful public dissent must not be dread of subjection to an unchecked surveillance power.

And in *Stanford v. Texas,* the Court emphasized that requirements of the Fourth Amendment are especially demanding when the protected freedoms of expression and association are involved. After reviewing the link between illegal searches and seizure and unpopular speech, the Court said:

This is the history which prompted the Court less than four years ago to remark that '[the] use by government of the power of search and seizure as an adjunct to a system for the suppression of objectionable publications is not new ... This history was, of course, part of the intellectual matrix within which our own constitutional fabric was shaped. The Bill of Rights was fashioned against the background of knowledge that unrestricted power of search and seizure could also be an instrument for stifling liberty of expression.' (Citations omitted)

Thus, whatever may be said about the soundness and continuing vitality of the *Hoffa* case, we need to remember the wise caution of Judge Learned Hand (in *United States v. Kirschenblatt*) that "what seems fair enough against a squalid huckster of bad liquor may take on a very different face, if used by a government determined to suppress political opposition under the guise of sedition."

Finally, in the non-political sphere we must also begin to recognize the dangers of an unchecked use of informers. As a beginning we have a right to demand of law enforcement authorities that their use of spies or informers should be confined to situations which generate probable cause that a target has committed, is engaged in or is about to engage in a criminal course of conduct and further to insist on limitations of time and place in order to avoid the transformation of the specifics demanded by the Fourth Amendment into a hunting license. See, "Judicial Control of Secret Agents," 76 Yale L.J. 994. Here too, I would urge that the policing of these limitations be confined, on the federal level at least, to the Attorney General and not to a court. We need to remember what recent events have tended to obscure: that under our system, the Attorney General is not only the nation's chief law enforcement officer, but a steward of our liberties. And beyond this, that while this may be a government of laws, the laws will be inoperative without good men to make them work.

THE RIGHT OF PRIVACY:
DATA BANKS AND DOSSIERS

by Arthur R. Miller

Professor of Law

Harvard University

In recent years there has been a growing public awareness of the effects certain data-gathering activities and applications of information technology may have on individual and commercial privacy. At times the debate has been conducted in emotional terms. For example, many people, myself included I must confess, have voiced the fear that the computer, with its insatiable appetite for information, its image of infallibility, and its inability to forget anything that has been put into it, may become the heart of a surveillance system that will turn society into a transparent world in which our home, our finances, and our associations are bared to the most casual observer.[1]

A brief recital of some of the blessings and blasphemies of the new technology makes the computer-privacy dilemma abundantly clear. In various medical centers, doctors are using computers to monitor physiological changes in the bodies of heart patients in the hope of isolating those alterations in body chemistry that precede a heart attack. The quest is to provide an "early warning system" so that treatment is not delayed until the actual heart attack has rendered the patient moribund for all practical purposes. Other plans include providing everyone with a number at birth to identify the individual for tax, banking, education, social security, and draft purposes. This would be done in conjunction with the computerization of a wide range of records. The goal is to eliminate much of the existing multiplicity in recordkeeping, and at the same time expedite the business of society. Long-range goals include developing a checkless, cashless economy, improving the informational bases available for rational planning, providing better services to people, and promoting the equitable allocation of society's resources. We may even see the day when if a person falls ill while away from home, a local doctor can use this identification number to retrieve the patient's medical history and drug reactions from a central data bank.

On the opposite side of the ledger, the same electronic sensors that can warn us of an impending heart attack also might be used to locate us, track our movements, and measure our emotions' and thoughts. Experiments already are underway in the field of telemetering and significant breakthroughs are on the horizon. The potential applications of this technology are staggering. I have heard it suggested that sensor implantation be made a condition of parole so that police can monitor the movements of those on probation. Similarly, the identification number given us at birth might become a leash around our necks and make us the object of constant monitoring, making credible the fear of the much fabled womb-to-tomb dossier. Finally, the administrative conveniences provided by the high degree of information centralization made possible through the widescale use of computers gives those who control the recordation and preservation of personal data a degree of power over us that is unprecedented and subject to potential abuse.[2]

Close scrutiny and evaluation of the implications of data technology and information systems on individual privacy have become especially appropriate because of the clarion in all quarters for the establishment of governmental and private data centers. For example, the United States Office of Education is supporting a migrant worker children data bank, the Department of Housing and Urban Development is sponsoring computerized municipal information systems and is building files on housing loan applicants (with particular attention given to those who are ineligible), and recent welfare reform proposals would give the Department of Health, Education and Welfare authority to exchange individualized data with state welfare agencies and might well lead to the establishment of a national job applicant data bank. In other areas, we are seeing the emergence of criminal intelligence data centers, such as the Federal Bureau of Investigation's National Crime Information Center (NCIC), and massive computer based credit and consumer reporting services.

Federal agencies and private companies are using computers and microfilm technology to collect, store, and exchange information about the activities of private citizens to an astounding degree. During the past few years we have read of the Department of Housing and Urban Development's Adverse Information File, the National Science Foundation's data bank on scientists, the Customs Bureau's computerized data bank on "suspects," the Civil Service Commission's "investigative" and "security" files, the Justice Department's intelligence bank run by that organization's civil disturbance group, the fact that files on millions of individuals are maintained by the Department of Transportation's National Driver Register Service, the Secret Service's dossiers on "undesirables," "activists," and "malcontents," and the surveillance activities of the United States Army. These are only some of the federal government's data banks that have been brought to light; even now only the tip of the iceberg may be visible.

Indeed, in light of these and numerous other data-gathering activities, I believe that Americans today are scrutinized, watched, counted, recorded, and questioned by more governmental agencies, social scientists, and law enforcement officials than at any other time in our history. Each time a citizen files a tax return, applies for life insurance or a credit card, seeks government benefits, or interviews for a job, a dossier is opened under his or her name and an informational profile is sketched. It has now reached the point at which, whenever we travel on a commercial airline, reserve a room at one of the national hotel chains, or rent a car, we are likely to leave distinctive electronic tracks in the memory of a computer — tracks that can tell a great deal about our activities, habits, and associations when collated and anlayzed. These fears are heightened by the regulations under a statute euphemistically titled the Bank Secrecy Act,[3] which require the microfilming of many of the checks we write and make them available to numerous investigators.

By and large, these data gathering activities are well-intended efforts to achieve socially desirable objectives. For example, in the law enforcement field, file-building is necessary to combat organized crime and restore "law and order." In a similar vein, the Federal Bureau of Investigation (FBI) and the Army can justify their intelligence activities in terms of combating subversion or quelling campus disruptions and riots in our urban centers by knowing who to watch or seize in times of strife. As to the information activities of credit grantors, private investigators, and insurance companies, which involve considerable snooping into an individual's private life in ways that often seem irrelevant to the purpose for which they are undertaken, it simply is good business to know as much as possible about a customer before you lend money, employ, or insure a life.

But there is a negative side to these mushrooming data banks — particularly those that bear the imprimatur of a governmental organization. Consider the information practices of the United States Army. Early in 1971, it was revealed that for some time Army intelligence units were systematically keeping watch on the *lawful* political activity of a number of groups and preparing "incident" reports and dossiers on individuals engaging in a wide range of *legal* protests. It must be emphasized that this monitoring not only covered society's "crazies" but included such nonviolent organizations as the National Association for the Advancement of Colored People (NAACP), the American Civil Liberties Union (ACLU), the Southern Christian Leadership Conference (SCLC), the Women's Strike for Peace, and allegedly extended to newsmen, congressmen, and a former governor.

Although there is considerable justification for certain types of information collection that are directly relevant to the Army's duties, the development of dossiers on people pursuing lawful social and political activities bears little relationship to the function of the military, even to its function during periods of social unrest. This especially is true when many of those being scrutinized are extremely unlikely to be involved in riotous conduct, and the selection of suspects seems to be governed by an incredibly simplistic these-are-the-good-guys-and-those-are-the-bad-guys approach. Not only is the Army's file-building difficult to justify, but it appears to have been undertaken without sufficient appreciation of the fact that the creation and exposure of dossiers on people who are politically active could deter them from exercising their rights to assemble, speak freely, dissent, or petition the government.

The development of other information systems in the law enforcement arena magnifies both the threat to personal privacy and the potential "chilling effect" of informational surveillance. The FBI's constantly expanding National Crime Information Center (prominently featured on the television series "The FBI") provides state and city police forces with immediate access to computerized files on many people. Although originally it contained only data on fugitives and stolen property, arrest records and other types of information have been added to the FBI system in recent years. Thus, the NCIC is the keystone of an emerging information network that will tie together the nation's law enforcement information centers. By the end of 1969, the Crime Information Center reportedly was exchanging data with state and local police agencies in every state except Alaska. Yet it was not until 1971 that the Department of Justice proposed rules for the governance of NCIC — rules that offer only a minimally effective privacy and security protection scheme.

State and local law enforcement surveillance systems also are becoming increasingly sophisticated — several with the aid of federal funding under the Law Enforcement Assistance Administration program of the Department of Justice. New York has the essential features of a network built around a simple computer center designed to store information for state and local agencies and permitting them to retrieve data through terminals placed throughout the state. An Ohio system allows dozens of agencies to share its computerized information and is connected both to NCIC and the Ohio State Highway Patrol computer center; plans are underway to tie it to comparable systems in Kentucky and Indiana. Fortunately, a number of state legislatures have recognized the potential abuse of these systems and protective legislation is in place in Alaska, Iowa, Massachusetts and Minnesota; other states undoubtedly will follow suit in the near future.

Unrestrained governmental recordkeeping poses a serious potential threat to values thought basic to the philosophical fibre of our society. If a citizen knows that his conduct and associations are being put "on file," and feels that there is some possibility that the information might be used to harass or injure, he may become more concerned about the possible content of that file and less willing to "stick his neck out" in pursuit of constitutional rights. The effect may be (to paraphrase a thought expressed by Justice Brennan in an analogous context) to encourage Americans to keep their mouths shut on all occasions.[4]

If we really take our constitutional guarantees seriously, we cannot afford to stand by and allow them to be debilitated by this type of coercion. Claims of governmental efficiency or the war against crime and subversion must not be allowed to justify every demand for gathering personal data. Because of the potential development of what might be called a "record prison" mentality, no one should be surprised at the suggestion that today's surveillance efforts contain the seeds of the much dreaded police state or a return to McCarthyism. Nor is it sufficient that governmental agencies assure us that surveillance and file-building are not being engaged in for repressive purposes. "Nineteen Eighty-Four" is largely a state of mind; for many, the appearance of repression has the impact of reality. If people really believe that recordkeeping is being used for nefarious purposes, it makes little difference that they may be wrong. They will still modify their perceptions of and behavior toward the institutions that control their files.

To prevent any doubt on the point, I do not oppose information systems or computerization of data. It strikes me as foolish to prevent the use of a modern technology to carry out important governmental and nongovernmental operations simply because it might be abused. This is especially true in our complex, urbanized, mass economy society, which desperately needs data for sound planning. We cannot turn the hands on the clock back. But this certainly does not justify inaction or complacency. There is a strong similarity between the difficulties that gave rise to the multifaceted regulation of airlines, automobiles, railroads, radio, and television and the problems that already are generating pressure for the comprehensive regulation of data banks and computer communications.

What is necessary at this time is the development of a framework for the protection of the public and the superimposition of that framework on information practices to minimize misuse of an otherwise socially desirable instrument. The problem of striking a balance between democracy and technology has been a frequent and manageable chore in the past and the nation's policy makers should not shrink from the task in this context.

I turn now to the particular tensions between contemporary data activities and privacy. Until recently, informational privacy has been relatively easy to protect for a number of reasons: (1) large quantities of information about individuals have not been available; (2) the available information generally has been decentralized; (3) the available information has been relatively superficial; (4) access to information has been difficult to secure; (5) people in a highly mobile society are difficult to keep track of; and (6) most people are unable to interpret and infer revealing information from data.

But these protections are part of a bygone era and are simply inapplicable to our technologically based society. Testimony before several committees of the United States Congress that have held hearings on various facets of privacy has revealed an astounding, and disheartening, panorama of the ways in which the intruders in our society, often aided by the fruits of modern science, have destroyed many of these traditional bastions of privacy.[5] Revelations concerning the widespread use of spike and parabolic microphones, a variety of gadgets for electronic eavesdropping, cameras equipped with modern optical devices that enable photographs to be taken at a distance and under adverse weather or light conditions, demonstrate that we do not necessarily enjoy physical privacy in our homes or offices, on the street, or — given the advent of the transistorized olive — while taking communion with a martini.

Now, ever increasing resort to the computer, laser technology, and microminiaturization techniques has begun to erode our informational privacy. Because the new technology makes it possible to integrate personal information from a variety of sources, solicitation lists increasingly are becoming the product of wide-ranging file investigations into the backgrounds and finances of prospective customers.[6] Personal information can be used for commercial purposes, such as generating a list of consumers with certain characteristics. READER'S DIGEST reportedly has used computer technology to produce a mailing list consisting of its subscribers' neighbors. "The approach had a kind of 'all the neighbors are doing it' quality," said one commentator. "But, more significantly, the individual was pleased that the READER'S DIGEST knew him and could relate him to others on his block."[7]

It should be evident to all that we live in an

increasingly information-based society. For example, ever since the federal government entered into the taxation and social welfare spheres, greater quantities of information have been sought from citizens and recorded. Moreover, in recent years access to governmental or institutional largesse — particularly in the welfare and Medicare-Medicaid contexts — increasingly has depended upon a willingness to divulge private information. As recording processes have become cheaper and more efficient, this data collection trend has intensified and been accompanied by a predilection toward centralization and collation. The effect is something akin to Parkinson's Law. As capacity for information handling has increased, there has been a tendency to engage in more extensive manipulation and analysis of recorded data, which in turn, has motivated the collection of data pertaining to a larger number of variables. The availability of electronic data storage and retrieval has accelerated this pattern, as evidenced by comparing the questions on a 1973 federal income tax form with those on a 1960 form and the significantly greater incidence of intrusive governmental, industrial, and academic questionnaires. It is now feasible to execute and evaluate these inquiries because of the availability of machine processing.

Accordingly, I think it is reasonable to assume that one consequence of the advent of data centers and increased computer capacity is that many governmental and private information gathering agencies will go beyond current levels of inquiry and begin to ask more complex, probing, and sensitive questions — perhaps into such subjects as associations with other people, location and activity at different points of time and space, medical history, and attitudes toward various institutions and persons. This trend already is being accelerated as a result of major federal social planning and resource allocation programs.

There are additional risks lurking in the ever-increasing reliance on recorded information and third-party evaluations of a person's past performance. As information cumulates, the contents of an individual's computerized dossier appear more and more impressive, despite the "softness" of much of the data, and impart to the user a heightened sense of reliability. Coupled with the myth of computer infallibility, this will make it less likely that an independent evaluation will be made or that the data will be verified. We are beginning to see more and more dependence on the files and the use of automatic criteria in the credit granting, insurance, educational, and employment fields.

I know a talented young lady who was unable to gain employment for some time following graduation from college because potential employers were wary of an entry in her university file that she became aware of only after many painful experiences. It said, "Melinda's mother is emotionally unstable." It turned out that this comment had been made by the girl's sixth grade teacher, who was neither a psychiatrist nor a psychologist and had only met the child's mother casually. Yet this damaging entry had been preserved and had followed Melinda for 15 years without anyone questioning either the propriety of its retention or its reliability or relevance.

Thus, not surprisingly, many people have come to feel that their success or failure in life ultimately may turn on what other people put into their file and on an unknown programmer's ability — or inability — to evaluate, process, and interrelate information. Moreover, as things now stand, a computerized file has a certain indelible quality — an old adversity or peccadillo cannot be overcome with time, absent an electronic eraser and a compassionate soul willing to use it.

The centralization of information from widely divergent sources also creates serious problems of information accuracy. This goes beyond the literal accuracy of what is recorded in the system, although that itself becomes a more serious problem as we increase the content of dossiers. Rather, I am concerned about the risks of using data out of context. Information can be entirely accurate and sufficient in one context and wholly incomplete and misleading in another. Computerization has made it convenient to rate an employee's efficiency and personal habits according to concise, conclusive categories such as "excellent," "fair," or "good" although different organizations often lack common traditions in appraising or interpreting performance.

The problem of contextual accuracy is best illustrated in terms of one of the most dangerous types of personal information in our society — the unexplained and incomplete arrest record. A very large percentage of the arrest records maintained and disseminated by police agencies in the United States, including those in the computerized criminal justice information systems described earlier, show no disposition of the charge following the arrest. For example, in Massachusetts, one out of five arrest records shows absolutely no subsequent judicial activity. How many more records contain entries relating to judicial activity but do not indicate the ultimate disposition of the proceeding — which might have been "no prosecution," "dismissed," "innocent," or "conviction reversed on appeal" — has not yet been ascertained. In a nation supposedly committed to the proposition that an accused is innocent until proven guilty, the maintenance and dissemination of incomplete arrest records, often to an audience far larger than the law enforcement community and to people who occasionally have little or no legitimate right to see them, is intolerable given the adverse impact they can have on the lives of file subjects.

Arrest records can be misleading even when they show disposition, especially when read by someone not trained, or inclined, to ask probing questions as to the meaning of the data. Is it likely that a citizen whose file contains an entry "arrested, 6/1/42; convicted felony, 1/6/43; sentenced, three years Leavenworth" will be given government employment or be accorded some of the other amenities of modern life? Yet our subject simply may have been a conscientious objector during the Second World War. Indeed, he may have been convicted under a standard that has since been invalidated as a violation of the constitutional right of freedom of religion. But note that the record neither makes the nature of the offense clear nor informs the reader of subsequent ameliorating facts.

Consider the potential effect of a computer entry "arrested, criminal trespass; sentenced, six months." Without elaboration how will the user know that our computerized person simply was demonstrating for equal employment in the North or desegregation in the South in the 1950's and was convicted under a statute that was overturned on appeal as an unconstitutional restraint on free speech, so that the subject is not a criminal at all? Will this individual be given the benefit of the presumption of innocence by the uninformed reader of the record?

In an era of great social activism on the part of the young, with counterpoint demands from others for "law and order," arrests are bound to increase. But many of them will be of a strikingly different character than what has been typical in the past. It is now common for hundreds of college demonstrators or social activists to be arrested in connection with one incident. Using recent experience as a guide, only a small fraction of the group will be prosecuted, and an even smaller number convicted. All of them, however, will have arrest records. Unless these records show disposition and are comprehensible, their circulation may have an unwarranted prejudicial effect.

And, make no mistake about it these records will circulate. In our information-crazy society, data about people is valuable, especially derogatory information. People will pay for it, or on occasion, steal it. We were warned of this when a number of consumer-reporting agencies — credit bureaus and detective agencies — entered a plea when they were prosecuted for bribing New York policemen to search fingerprint and arrest records for them. In addition, there is what might be called the "information buddy system." It is a striking fact that many, if not most, bank or corporate security officers, private detectives, insurance and credit bureau investigators are former federal or local law enforcement agents who, by maintaining past associations, still have the ability to gain access to criminal justice and fiscal information systems.

It also seems reasonable to assume that the desirability of getting at a data center's extensive store of information will offset the difficulties of gaining access to computerized files and deciphering them, which occasionally are offered as reasons why machine readable information is inherently more secure than manually-stored data. Even if we assume that the cost of securing access to computerized secure than manually-stored data. Even if we assume that the cost of securing access to computerized "dirt" is higher than the cost of dredging out the "dirt" in a more traditional form of record, the centralized quality and compactness of a computerized dossier creates an incentive to invade it because the payoff for doing so successfully may be sufficiently large that the cost per unit of computerized "dirt" actually will prove to be lower than the cost per unit of uncomputerized "dirt."

It should not be forgotten that the risks to privacy created by data centers lie not only in abuse of the system by those who desire to injure others or who can obtain some personal advantage by doing so. There is a legitimate fear of over-centralizing individualized information and then expanding the number of people who, by having access to it, also have the capacity to inflict damage through negligence, sloppiness, and sheer stupidity. Unthinking people are as capable of injuring others by unintentionally rendering a record inaccurate, losing it, or disseminating its contents to unauthorized people, as are people acting out of malice or for personal aggrandizement.

What then is the solution? As an initial matter, one would hope that good judgment and self-regulation on the part of the information-gathering and using communities would suffice. Those who handle individualized data — whether it be in the context of financial profiles in a credit bureau, student records in a school system, medical files in a hospital, welfare lists in a government agency, or personal data in a large corporation — have an obligation to guard the privacy of the human beings whose lives are reflected in those dossiers. But we must also come to grips with a basic fact of life concerning computerized information systems. The only completely effective guardian of individual privacy is the imposition of *strict* controls over the information that can be collected, stored, and disseminated. No procedural or technical safeguard is immune from human abuse or mechanical failure.

Certain types of information should not be recorded, even if it is technically feasible to do so and some administrative objective would be served thereby. It has long been technically "feasible" and, from some perspectives, "desirable" to require citizens to carry and display passports when moving through the country, or to require universal finger-printing. But the United States has not pursued these objectives because they are considered inconsistent with the democratic tradition of our society, although the proliferating use of the Social Security number may produce a *de facto* universal identifier whether we like it or not. By the same token absent an overpowering demonstration that the preservation of sensitive or highly personal information, such as medical and psychiatric information, or dossier-type information on those pursuing lawful political and social activities, is essential to some

fundamental policy, the scrivener's hand should be stayed and the data permitted to be lost to man's memory or simply retained on a decentralized and highly confidential basis.

Another form of self-regulation that seems essential is limiting access to data. The hardware and software of any system dealing with personalized information should be designed to limit the exposure of files to a limited class of people, whose access is authorized only after a careful examination of their need to know. The identity of everyone making an inquiry into an individual file must be required before access is permitted. But it must be remembered that an identification code number assigned to each user or a magnetically coded identification card easily can be lost, stolen, or exchanged. Thus, ultimately, finger or voice prints may prove to be necessary. In addition, the system should be equipped with protector files to record the identity of inquirers and these records should be audited periodically to determine whether the system is being misused by those who have a legitimate right of access. In the same vein, it probably will be necessary to audit the programs controlling the manipulation of the files to make sure that no one has inserted a secret "door" in the protective software or modified it so that a particular password will permit access to the data by unauthorized personnel.

Because it is possible to move information into or out of a computer over substantial distances by telephone lines or microwave relays connected to terminals scattered throughout the country and even beyond, it is essential that information be protected against wiretapping and other forms of electronic eavesdropping. This risk can be minimized by coding the data or using "scramblers" to garble the information before transmission and installing complementary devices in the authorized terminals to reconstitute the signal. These procedures also will prevent "piggy-backing" or "infiltrating" the system by surreptitiously attaching a terminal to an authorized user's transmission line.

To insure the accuracy of computerized files, an individual should have access to any information in his dossier and an opportunity to challenge its accuracy. This principle has been recognized and is embodied in a recent federal statute—the Fair Credit Reporting Act.[8] This enactment is the first step toward eliminating some of the abuses in the buying and selling of personal information by consumer reporting companies, most notably credit bureaus. It give individuals a right of access to the files maintained by these organizations, provides a procedure for correcting any errors that are found, assures us of notice when adverse decisions are made on the basis of a consumer report, and places some restraints on the investigative reporting conducted by these firms. Although the act is extremely porous, its basic philosophical premise—that an individual has a right to see his or her file—is sound and must be extended to other contexts. Fortunately, this appears to be happening in the criminal justice field with regard to criminal offender record information.

Another approach might be to send a person's record to him once a year or to notify each file subject of the existence of the file and the right to gain access to it, as well as to correct any inaccuracies that might be found. This suggestion may prove expensive. Some will argue that the value of certain information will be damaged if its existence is disclosed; also it might produce a flow of petty squabbles that would entail costly and debilitating administrative or judicial proceedings. Nevertheless, the right of an individual to be protected against the dissemination of misinformation about him is so important that some price must be paid to effectuate it and meaningful notice seems to be a basic ingredient of an effective privacy program.

Finally, the information must not be allowed to petrify. Data that is shown to be inaccurate, or archaic, or of little probative value, should be deleted, reclassified, or its age brought to the attention of a user of the file.

But what if self-regulation fails? Indeed, can we afford the luxury of waiting to find out? It seems clear to me that the solution to the computer-privacy dilemma lies in the enforcement of the principles just outlined by legislation, administrative regulation, and the judicial process. Unfortunately, we cannot be too sanguine about the existing legal structure's ability to meet the challenge without affirmative action being taken by Congress and various federal agencies. The common law of privacy traditionally has been preoccupied with the problems raised by the mass media and has concerned itself with the commercial exploitation

of a name or likeness, the offensive intrusion into an individual's personal affairs, the widespread public disclosure of private information, and the "false light" cast on individuals by media disclosures.[9] These doctrines are of no value in meeting the challenge of the computer.

In the constitutional law arena, cases seeking the expungement of files maintained by law enforcement agencies only have been partially successful, despite strong arguments that the preservation of detailed information directly infringes the data subject's right of associated privacy under the First Amendment.[10] Relief usually has been denied because of a judicial concern over the government's need to deal effectively with lawlessness. Furthermore, any privacy action based on constitutional rights will have to avoid the inhibiting effect of the Supreme Court's decision in *Time, Inc. v. Hill*,[11] which imposes an extremely heavy burden of proof on the party seeking relief for an invasion of privacy.[12] The effect of that case is to give the media substantial immunity from liability for invasions of privacy in order to provide "breathing space" for freedom of expression. I think it is fair to say that the *Hill* decision partially abborts the common law right of privacy's capacity for doctrinal growth, although a recent decision of the Supreme Court in the doctrinally related area of defamation offers some amelioration.[13]

The judicial vineyards are not completely blighted, however. The constitutional right of associational privacy is probably the most clearly developed of the constitutional protections for personal information. Thus, when the government attempts to gather data from an individual concerning his association with a group dedicated to the advancement of certain beliefs, it must show that the information sought is a subject of overriding and compelling state interest.[14] Closely related to associational privacy is another type of privacy that the courts have protected—the right to possess ideas and beliefs free from governmental intrusion. The leading case in this area, *Schneider v. Smith*,[15] makes it clear that espousing an unpopular idea is not a scar a person must display upon inquiry for the remainder of one's life.

A related line of cases protects our physical privacy from unreasonable searches and seizures and guarantees us the "right to be let alone" in what have been described as "zones of privacy."[16] This view is exemplified by *Griswold v. Connecticut*,[17] which struck down Connecticut's attempt to regulate the use of contraceptive devices. The precise basis for the *Griswold* result is obscure because the seven justices comprising the majority wrote four opinions and no more than three justices could agree on any one theory. According to Mr. Justice Douglas' opinion, there are certain rights not enumerated in the Bill of Rights, including a right of privacy, that can be found in the "penumbra" of those expressly guaranteed by the Constitution. Unfortunately, once he decided that privacy was a constitutional right, the Justice simply concluded that the marital relationship is "within the zone of privacy."[18] In a concurring opinion by Mr. Justice Goldberg, joined by Chief Justice Warren and Mr. Justice Brennan, emphasis was placed on the Ninth Amendment.[19] In a separate opinion, Mr. Justice Harlan invoked notions of substantive due process and characterized the right of privacy as a "liberty" within the meaning of the Fourteenth Amendment.[20] A similar approach was taken by Mr. Justice White, although he declined to refer to it as a "right of privacy" preferring to think of it as a specific protected "liberty."[21]

The Supreme Court's next pronouncement in the privacy field was *Stanley v. Georgia*,[22] in which the Court struck down a state statute that proscribed the possession of obscene material in the home. The opinion seems to be based on a combination of First Amendment and sanctity-of-the-home concerns. *Stanley*, however, has been limited by later decisions treating it as a case involving privacy of the home and little else.[23] Moreover, a more recent Supreme Court decision, upholding the right of the state welfare authorities to terminate benefits if they are denied access to the welfare recipient's home under certain circumstances, seems to look away from an expansive view of privacy.[24]

On the other hand, in *Eisenstadt v. Baird*,[25] the Court extended the *Griswold* decision to invalidate a Massachusetts statute that prohibited the distribution of contraceptives to unmarried persons. Speaking for the Court, Mr. Justice Brennan rejected any distinction between the state's power to regulate contraception among married and unmarried persons as a violation of the equal protection clause.

According to the Court: "If the right of privacy means anything, it is the right of the individual, married or single, to be free from unwarranted governmental intrusion into matters so fundamentally affecting a person as the decision whether to bear or beget a child."[26]

The Supreme Court's most recent and most significant pronouncement regarding the constitutional status of the right to privacy is *Roe v. Wade*,[27] in which this right unequivocally is stated to be the basis for limiting state power to criminalize abortions. According to Mr. Justice Blackmun:

The right of privacy, whether it be founded in the Fourteenth Amendment's concept of personal liberty and restrictions upon state action, as we feel it is, or, as the District Court determined, in the Ninth Amendment's reservation of rights to the people, is broad enough to encompass a woman's decision whether or not to terminate her pregnancy.[28]

The plaintiff in *Roe* was an unmarried pregnant woman and the decision seems to be a clear recognition of the right of an individual to control certain decisions related to his or her own life or body. In effect, the Court concluded that the state must have a compelling interest to justify any limitations on a "fundamental" right that is an aspect of the Fourteenth Amendment.

But are these decisions about contraception, pornography, and abortion relevant to the law of privacy in the field of recordkeeping? Is the right to control information about onself—particularly the right to decide when to go public with personal data—a "fundamental" right that is "implicit in the concept of ordered liberty"?[29] Even if the answer to this query is yes, under what circumstances is the state's interest in collecting or using information about an individual "compelling"? In sum, there is still a long decisional path to be traversed before a constitutional right of *informational* privacy is established.

The courts have not been inclined to conclude that the collection of personal information by the government is a violation of a constitutional right; even though, these cases generally involve situations in which there is a clear, valid justification for the particular governmental information activity.[30] This has been the attitude of the courts even when the personal information is released to the public.[31] Not surprisingly, therefore, one commentator, unfortunately without analysis or a considered explanation, has suggested that the right to control personal information should be distinguished from the "right of autonomous decision" that he believes is at the root of *Griswold and Roe*.[32] It remains to be seen whether the courts will draw that distinction.

A few recent cases do suggest that the Supreme Court decisions described above may have some relevance in the recordkeeping arena. For example, a New York court in *Schulman v. New York City Health & Hospitals Corp.*,[33] struck down a regulation requiring the identification on fetal death certificates of women who had undergone abortions; a violation of the constitutional right of privacy was the basis for the decision. The court seemed to be concerned about the stigma that might attach to a woman—particularly an unmarried woman— who had undergone an abortion and felt that the need for secrecy was essential to effectuate the right to have an abortion. None of the State's asserted countervailing policies was found persuasive. Similarly, the United States Court of Appeals for the Second Circuit has indicated that the New York Controlled Substances Act, which requires the disclosure of certain personal information, presents a significant constitutional privacy problem.[34] Finally, there are cases relying on *Griswold* that recognize a right of privacy in connection with arrest records which are maintained even though the accused has been acquitted or the charges against him have been dropped.[35]

Very little comfort for those seeking an expanded constitutional right of privacy based on the *Roe* case is provided by the Supreme Court's very recent decision in *California Bankers' Association v. Schultz*,[36] in which a broad attack on the Bank Secrecy Act of 1970[37] under the First, Fourth, Fifth, Ninth, Tenth, and Fourteenth Amendments, failed. The suit attacked the U.S. Treasury Department's regulations under that statute, which require banks to maintain records relating to the financial activities of their customers, including the microfilming and retention of copies of all checks in excess of $100, and the automatic reporting to the government of all large domestic and foreign currency transactions above certain

dollar amounts. Mr. Justice Rehnquist, in an opinion joined by three other members of the Court,[38] sequentially rejected each of the challenger's points. Summarizing, he concluded that the recordkeeping requirements did not create an unreasonable burden on banks so as to violate due process; that the obligation to maintain the records, as opposed to a requirement to turn them over to the government, was not an invasion of the prohibition against unreasonable searches and seizures; that the banks, having no privilege against self-incrimination, could not raise that objection; that the assertion the recordkeeping might be used by governmental investigators to identify members of organizations in violation of the First Amendment right of freedom of association was premature; that the Fourth Amendment challenges to the reporting requirements failed because the statutory purposes were reasonable and the depositor plaintiffs lacked standing to challenge the domestic reporting regulations; that the banks could not challenge the reporting requirements on the ground of self-incrimination and that the depositor plaintiffs' similar attack on the reporting requirements was premature; and, finally, that the ACLU's claim that its associational freedom under the First Amendment was violated was premature. The Court's opinion never mentions the possible relevancy of the constitutional right of privacy; nor does it cite *Griswold* or *Roe*.

Mr. Justice Powell and Mr. Justice Blackmun interposed a short concurring opinion suggesting that they might not have joined in the result if the Treasury Department's regulations had applied to all banking transactions.[39] Separate dissents were filed by Mr. Justice Douglas,[40] Mr. Justice Brennan,[41] and Mr. Justice Marshall.[42] Only Mr. Justice Douglas' opinion directly addressed the privacy implications of the regulations; the other two dissenters merely indicated general agreement with his remarks. However, although Mr. Justice Douglas strongly attacked the "Big Brother" aspects of the recordkeeping requirements, he did not suggest any possible constitutional dimension to the privacy aspects of the Bank Secrecy Act regulations and only made a general footnote reference to the *Roe* case.

Despite the Supreme Court's silence with regard to the possible relevance of the constitutional right of privacy, the *California Bankers'* case undoubtedly will have a depressant effect on the extension of *Griswold* and *Roe* to informational privacy. The Court's willingness to accept Congress' statement of purpose and need for the record-keeping and reporting regulations, as well as its judgment that they were immune from a range of constitutional challenges, suggests a lack of receptivity on the part of the Court to challenges to governmental data practices that have a plausible sounding justification.

Another theory that might be used to raise the privacy aspects of recordkeeping to constitutional dimensions is based on the argument that, even if the right to control personal information is not part of the constitutional privacy right envisioned in *Griswold* and *Roe*, it nonetheless should be protected under previously discarded substantive due process principles that may have been revitalized by these cases.[43] It seems reasonable to infuse due process notions into the use of information by requiring that a minimal level of procedural fairness be satisfied when a person's reputation, financial position, or integrity is jeopardized by a governmental dissemination of personal information. In this connection, mention should be made of *Wisconsin v. Constantineau*.[44] If given an expansive reading, this case seems to suggest that governmental institutions must afford procedural fairness in the gathering, utilization, and dissemination of personal information. However, factual peculiarities in *Constantineau* caution against expecting too much from it in future cases.

It is important to realize that all of the judicial decisions described above simply represent an attempt to define the outer boundaries or constitutional limits on governmental action—they do not give us any guidance in establishing the standard for achieving the desperately needed balance between data collection and individual rights. Moreover, they are not applicable to limiting information activities in the private sphere. More sensitive and comprehensive regulation will have to come from the legislature or administrative agencies.

A number of Congressmen—perhaps encouraged by some of the privacy-related aspects of Watergate—already have recognized the need for some statutory controls and have introduced legislation to protect privacy. Unfortunately, the activity is somewhat reminiscent of Leacock's Man,

who jumped on his horse and rode off in all directions at once. Bills have appeared to regulate credit bureaus, arrest records, mailing list companies, the census, employee privacy, government inquiries, the Social Security number, and psychological testing. Thus far, only the Fair Credit Reporting Act, mentioned earlier, has been enacted into law. But Senators Ervin and Percy and Congressmen Goldwater and Koch have proposed extensive regulation of information systems and data gathering practices that are under active consideration as of this writing.

There also is considerable activity in this field at the state level, with a number of provisions near enactment and commissions, studying the problem in several jurisdictions. Given the political attractiveness of the privacy issue at this time, the pressure for legislative actions is likely to continue and bear considerable fruit.

Virtually all of the current legislative proposals follow one of two basic models. The first, which is based upon recommendations in the seminal report of a U.S. Department of Health, Education and Welfare Special Committee on Automated Personal Data Systems entitled, *Records, Computers, and the Rights of Citizens*, would create a standard of fair information practices that must be honored by data gatherers and users. It also provides data subjects with various procedural rights to help insure the integrity of files relating to them. Enforcement of the legislation largely would depend on private civil actions brought by individual file subjects.

The second, which seems to derive from Sweden's Data Protection Act, also establishes standards of conduct and individual rights. It goes further, however, and establishes a regulatory authority with rulemaking and enforcement powers. An attempt has been made by the draftsman to make this body independent of those having interests in the data and its use. The notion of an independent information agency is not a new one. Many of the congressional witnesses and commentators on the proposal to create a National Data Center stressed the importance of locating control of such an organization *outside* the existing regulatory framework.[45] Ongoing administrative regulation would obviate the risk of making highly detailed policy judgments in statutory form prematurely. It also would guarantee that the problem is placed in the hands of a watchdog group, hopefully composed of experts drawn from many fields, that could exercise continuing supervision over the data handling community.[46]

Proposals differ in terms of whether they apply to private, as well as governmental, systems and whether they extend only to automated, or both automated and manual systems. They also vary as to the detail with which the standards imposed on data users are spelled out. Congressmen Goldwater and Koch have prepared an omnibus proposal containing features drawn from both models, and there is substantial support in both houses for it.[47] It would apply to all personal information systems, limit the permissible range of organizational data collection, fully inform the individual as to the nature of an information request at the time it is made, impose a code of professional secrecy on information handlers, limit demands for the Social Security number, require annual public notice by organizations using personal information, enable the individual to secure a copy of his file, establish a full-time federal privacy board with powers to regulate, conduct research, and inspect systems, and authorize the courts to impose civil and criminal penalties. The Koch-Goldwater Bill exempts criminal law enforcement, national defense, and press files, loopholes that could undermine its effectiveness.

When the dust ultimately settles, I hope we have struck an appropriate balance between society's need for information and the individual's need in a democracy for privacy. This probably will require give on both sides. No doubt we can coerce, wheedle, and cajole an individual into giving up part, or even all, of his informational profile. But what price would we pay for it? Alienation, distrust of the government, deceptive responses, obfuscation of certain data gathering objectives (as I think may have happened to the original census goal of enumerating the population), numbing of privacy values, and an atmosphere of suspicion. Governmental and private planners must refine their information handling techniques, reduce the data extraction burden on the individual, and assure us of file accuracy and security against improper dissemination. If this is done, perhaps we will feel less apprehensive about yielding a little of ourselves.

Few aspects of life, even in a free society, can survive as absolutes—and that includes privacy.

In any event, it is essential to counteract the syndrome referred to by the poet e.e. cummings, when he wrote "progress is a comfortable disease."[48] We must overcome the all-to-often complacent attitude of citizens toward the management of our affairs by what frequently are astigmatic administrators in both government and the private sector. The very real benefits conferred by information technology may opiate our awareness of the price that may be exacted in terms of personal freedom. It thus seems desirable to sound the Klaxon to arouse a greater awareness of the possibility that the computer is precipitating a realignment in the patterns of societal power and is becoming an increasingly important decision-making tool in practically all of our significant governmental and nongovernmental institutions. As society becomes more and more information oriented, the central issue that emerges to challenge us is how to contain the excesses and channel the benefits of this new form of power.

If the concept of personal privacy is fundamental to our tradition of individual autonomy, and if its preservation is deemed desirable, then we must overcome inertia. Otherwise, there will be no one to blame but ourselves if some day we discover that the mantle of policymaking is being worn by those specially trained technicians who have found the time to master the machine and are using it for their own purposes. To paraphrase the French sociologist, Jacques Ellul, that it is to be a dictatorship of dossiers and data banks rather than of hobnailed boots will not make it any less a dictatorship.[49]

———————

Notes to
THE RIGHT TO PRIVACY: DATA BANKS AND DOSSIERS
by Arthur R. Miller

The author has explored the subject matter of his paper more fully in A. Miller, *The Assault on Privacy: Computers, Data Banks, and Dossiers* (1971), and Miller, *Personal Privacy in the Computer Age: The Challenge of a New Technology in an Information-Oriented Society,* 67 Mich. L. Rev. 1089 (1969).

1.   Miller, *The National Data Center and Personal Privacy,* The Atlantic, Nov. 1967, at 53-57.

2.   *Dombrowski v. Pfister,* 380 U.S. 479, 487, 85 S. Ct. 1116, 1121 (1965).

3.   Pub. L. No. 91-508, 84 Stat. 1114, 12 U.S.C. §§ 18296b, 1730d, 1951-1959, 31 U.S.C. §§ 1051-1122 (1970).

4.   *Lopez v. United States,* 373 U.S. 427, 450, 83 S. Ct. 1381, 1393-94 (1963) (dissenting opinion).

5.   See generally Hearings on Federal Data Banks and the Bill of Rights Before the Subcomm. on Constitutional Rights of the Comm. on the Judiciary, 91st Cong., 1st Sess. (1971); Hearings on Commercial Credit Bureaus Before a Subcomm. of the House Comm. on Government Operations, 90th Cong., 2d Sess. (1968); Hearings on Computer Privacy Before the Subcomm. on Administrative Practice and Procedure of the Senate Comm. on the Judiciary, 90th Cong., 2d Sess. (1968); Hearings on the Coordination and Integration of Government Statistical Programs Before the Subcomm. on Economic Statistics of the Joint Economic Comm., 90th Cong., 1st Sess. (1967); Hearings on the Computer and Invasion of Privacy Before a Subcomm. of the House Comm. on Government Operations, 89th Cong., 2d Sess. (1966).

6.   See A. Miller, *The Assault on Privacy: Computers, Data Banks, and Dossiers* 79-85 (1971).

7.   *New York Times,* July 30, 1968, at 41, col. 1.

8.   Pub. L. No. 91-508, 84 Stat. 1127-36, 15 U.S.C. §§ 1601-77, 1681-1681t (1970).

9.   See A. Miller, *supra* note 6, at 173-89.

10.   See *Anderson v. Sills,* 56 N.J. 210, 265 A.2d 678 (1970), reversing 106 N.J. Super. 545, 256 A.2d 298 (1969). But compare *Sullivan v. Murphy,* 478 F.2d 938 (D.C. Cir. 1973), certiorari denied 94 S. Ct. 162 (1973); *Menard v. Mitchell,* 430 F.2d 486 (D.C. Cir. 1970). Judge Gesell's opinion on remand in the *Menard* case reflects a very balanced and sophisticated approach to the data bank question. *Menard v. Mitchell,* 328 F.Supp. 718 (D. D.C. 1971).

11.   385 U.S. 374, 87 S. Ct. 534 (1967).

12.   See A. Miller, *supra* note 6, at 190-99.

13.   *Gertz v. Robert Welch, Inc.,* – U.S. ____, 94 S. Ct. 2997 (1974).

14.   See *NAACP v. Alabama,* 357 U.S. 449, 78 S. Ct. 1163 (1958). See also *Gibson v. Florida Legislative Investigation Comm.,* 372 U.S. 539, 83 S. Ct. 889 (1963).

15.   390 U.S. 17, 88 S. Ct. 682 (1968).

16.   See *Stanley v. Georgia,* 394 U.S. 557, 89 S. Ct. 1243 (1969); *Katz v. United States,* 389 U.S. 347, 350 n.5, 88 S. Ct. 507, 510-11 n.5 (1967); *Berger v. New York,* 388 U.S. 41, 87 S. Ct. 1873 (1967).

17.   381 U.S. 479, 85 S. Ct. 1678 (1965).

18.   Id. at 485, 85 S. Ct. at 1682.

19.   Id. at 486-99, 85 S. Ct. at 1682-90.

20.   Id. at 499-502, 85 S. Ct. at 1690-91.

21.   Id. at 502-07, 85 S. Ct. at 1691-94.

22.   394 U.S. 557, 89 S. Ct. 1243 (1969).

23.   See, e.g., *Paris Adult Theatre I v. Slaton,* 413 U.S. 49, 93 S. Ct. 2628 (1973).

24.   *Wyman v. James,* 400 S. Ct. 309, 91 S. Ct. 381 (1971). See generally Burt, *Forcing Protection on Children and Their Parents: The Impact of Wyman v. James,* 69 Mich. L. Rev. 1259 (1971). See also *Law Students Civil Rights Research Council, Inc. v. Wadmond,* 401 U.S. 154, 91 S. Ct. 744 (1971).

25.   405 U.S. 438, 92 S. Ct. 1029 (1972).

26.   Id. at 453, 92 S. Ct. at 1038.

27.   410 U.S. 113, 93 S. Ct. 705 (1973).

28.   Id. at 153, 93 S. Ct. at 727.

29. *Palko v. Connecticut,* 302 U.S. 319, 325, 58 S. Ct. 149, 152 (1937). This passage was relied upon by the Court in *Roe v. Wade,* 410 U.S. 113, 152-53, 93 S. Ct. 705, 706 (1973).

30. E.g., *Cantor v. Supreme Court of Pennsylvania,* 353 F.Supp. 1307, 1321-22 (E.D.Pa. 1973); *Thom v. New York Stock Exchange,* 306 F.Supp. 1002 (S.D.N.Y 1969), affirmed per curiam sub nom. *Miller v. New York Stock Exchange,* 425 F.2d 1074 (2d Cir.), certiorari denied, 398 U.S. 905 (1970). See also *Winters v. Miller,* 446 F.2d 65 (2d Cir. 1971) (fingerprinting).

31. E.g., *Tosh v. Buddies Supermarkets, Inc.,* 482 F.2d 329 (5th Cir. 1973) (release of arrest records); *Rosenberg v. Martin,* 478 F.2d 520, 524-25 (2d Cir. 1973), certiorari denied, 414 U.S. 872 (1973) (information about fugitive given to the news media); *Lamont v. Commissioner of Motor Vehicles,* 269 F.Supp. 880 (S.D.N.Y.), affirmed per curiam, 386 F.2d 449 (2d Cir. 1967), certiorari denied, 391 U.S. 915 (1968) (sale of motor vehicle registration records).

32. Note, *On Privacy: Constitutional Protections for Personal Liberty,* 48 N.Y.U.L.Rev. 670, 770-72 (1973).

33. 70 M.2d 1093, 335 N.Y.S.2d 343 (Sup. Ct. 1972), vacated and remanded, 41 A.D.2d 714, 341 N.Y.S.2d 242 (1st Dep't), judgment reinstated, 75M.2d 150, 346 N.Y.S.2d 920 (Sup. Ct. 1973).

34. *Roe v. Ingraham,* 480 F.2d 102, 107-08 (2d Cir. 1973), on remand, 364 F.Supp. 536 (S.D.N.Y. 1973) (preliminary injunction denied for failure to demonstrate that the competing interests of the state do not outweigh the injury plaintiffs might suffer). See also *Merriken v. Cressman,* 364 F.Supp. 913 (E.D.Pa. 1973) (drug abuse problem held to violate constitutional right of privacy).

35. E.g., *Davidson v. Dill,* Colo., 503 P. 2d 157 (1972) (dismissal of action to expunge arrest record of person who was acquitted held improper); *Eddy v. Moore,* 5 Wash. App. 334, 487 P. 2d 211 (1971) (same). Some courts have not relied on the constitutional right of privacy. See, e.g., *Sullivan v. Murphy,* 478 F.2d 938 (D.C. Cir. 1973), certiorari denied 94 S. Ct. 162 (1973); *Hughes v. Rizzo,* 282 F.Supp. 881 (E.D. Pa. 1968); *United States v. Kalish,* 271 F. Supp. 968 (D. Puerto Rico 1967). See also *Menard v. Mitchell,* 430 F.2d 486 (D.C.Cir. 1970).

36. ____ U.S. ____, 94 S. Ct. 1494 (1974).

37. Public Law No. 91-508, 84 Stat. 1114, 12 U.S.C. §§ 1829b, 1730d, 1951-1959, 31 U.S.C. §§ 1051-1122 (1970).

38. Id. at 4498.

39. Id. at 4499.

40. Id. at 4502.

41. Id. at 4503.

42. Id. at 4501 n. 7.

43. Further evidence of the rebirth of substantive due process is found in *Cleveland Board of Education v. La Fleur,* ____ U.S.____, 94 S. Ct. 791 (1974), which invalidated state regulations requiring pregnant school teachers to take a maternity leave after five months of pregnancy. The Supreme Court did not appear to rely on privacy for its result.

44. 400 U.S. 433, 91 S. Ct. 507 (1971).

45. See Hearings on Computer Privacy Before the Subcomm. on Administrative Practice and Procedure of the Senate Comm. on the Judiciary, 90th Cong., 2d Sess. (1968) (statement of Professor Arthur R. Miller); Note, *Privacy and Efficient Government: Proposals for a National Data Center,* 82 Harv. L. Rev. 400, 404 (1968). See also Ruggles, *On the Needs and Values of Data Banks, in Symposium—Computers, Data Banks, and Individual Privacy,* 53 Minn. L. Rev. 211, 218-19 (1963); Zwick, *A National Data Center, in* A.B.A. Section of Individual Rights and Responsibilities, Monograph No. 1, at 32, 33 (1967).

46. This theme is developed in A. Miller, *supra* note 6, at 228-38.

47. H.R. 14163, 93d Cong., 2d Sess. (1974).

48. e.e. cummings, *100 Selected Poems* 89 (paperback ed. 1959).

49. J. Ellul, *The Technological Society* 434 (paperback ed. 1964).

ANNUAL CHIEF JUSTICE EARL WARREN CONFERENCE ON ADVOCACY IN THE UNITED STATES / 1974

HERBERT H. BENNETT
President
Roscoe Pound-American Trial Lawyers Foundation

THEODORE I. KOSKOFF
Chairman
Annual Chief Justice Earl Warren Conference
on Advocacy

Background Papers

PROFESSOR HERMAN SCHWARTZ
State University of New York
at Buffalo School of Law

Subject: REFLECTIONS ON SIX YEARS
OF LEGITIMATED ELECTRONIC SURVEILLANCE

FRANK J. DONNER, ESQ.
Director, American Civil Liberties Union
Project on Political Surveillance
Yale Law School

Subject: POLITICAL INTELLIGENCE: CAMERAS,
INFORMERS AND FILES

PROFESSOR ARTHUR R. MILLER
Harvard University Law School

Subject: THE RIGHT OF PRIVACY: DATA BANKS
AND DOSSIERS

Group Chairmen

DR. EDWARD J. BLOUSTEIN
President, Rutgers University, The State University of New Jersey; formerly President of Bennington College, Bennington, Vermont; Law professor

DR. NORMAN FREDERIKSEN
Director of Division of Psychological Studies, Educational Testing Service; former Professor of Psychology, Princeton University

PROFESSOR H. RICHARD UVILLER
Professor, Columbia University School of Law and Attorney practicing in criminal matters; former Assistant District Attorney In Charge of Appeals Bureau, New York County; author of forthcoming two-volume casebook on criminal process

Group Rapporteurs

NAT HENTOFF
Journalist; co-author of recent book, "State Secrets - Police Surveillance in America"

PROFESSOR L. THORNE MC CARTY
Assistant Professor, Faculty of Law and Jurisprudence, State University of New York at Buffalo; previously Law and Computer Fellow at Stanford Law School and also lecturer in law; developed and conducted courses on technology and law both at Stanford and State University of New York

PROFESSOR GARY T. MARX
Associate Professor, Department of Urban Studies and Planning (sociology), Massachusetts Institute of Technology; Senior Research Associate, Center for Criminal Justice, Harvard Law School; area of interest includes civil rights issues – riots, disorder, police, black/white race relations in America

Conferees

DR. EDWARD J. BLOUSTEIN
New Brunswick, New Jersey
President, Rutgers University, The State University of New Jersey; formerly President of Bennington College, Bennington, Vermont; Law professor

SARAH COLLINS CAREY
Washington, D.C.
Partner, Gore, Cladouhos & Brashares; formerly Assistant Director for National Projects, Lawyers' Committee for Civil Rights Under Law working at law reform in school finance, manpower and employment problems, state and local government and federal criminal justice programs

KENNETH CONBOY
New York, New York
Assistant District Attorney In Charge of the Rackets Bureau, County of New York (Manhattan), has served in this Office for seven years, Senior Trial Assistant

ROBERT H. COURTNEY, JR.
Poughkeepsie, New York
Manager, Data Security and Privacy, International Business Machines Corporation; established architectural and design criteria for data security in IBM's hardware and software

DR. RUTH M. DAVIS
Washington, D.C.
> Director, Institute for Computer Sciences and Technology, National Bureau of Standards, U.S. Department of Commerce; active in several fields of computer information processing technology such as control systems, computer networks and automation

ROBERT J. DEL TUFO
Trenton, New Jersey
> First Assistant Attorney General, State of New Jersey, served as Assistant Prosecutor, Morris County, New Jersey

PROFESSOR JOHN T. ELLIFF
Waltham, Massachusetts
> Assistant Professor, Department of Politics, Brandeis University; former Assistant Professor, Department of Political Science, Barnard College, Columbia University; his work includes research on the Justice Department and the Federal Bureau of Investigation

PROFESSOR THOMAS I. EMERSON
New Haven, Connecticut
> Lines Professor of Law, Yale Law School; a constitutional theoretician of national stature, Professor Emerson's scholarly works include "The System of Freedom of Expression" and "Toward a General Theory of the First Amendment"

DR. ROBERT M. FANO
Cambridge, Massachusetts
> Ford Professor of Engineering, Department of Electrical Engineering, Massachusetts Institute of Technology; organized and directed Project MAC, MIT's leading computer research laboratory for five years

DR. NORMAN FREDERIKSEN
Princeton, New Jersey
> Director of Division of Psychological Studies, Educational Testing Service; former Professor of Psychology, Princeton University

ALFRED M. FREEDMAN, M.D.
New York, New York
> President, American Psychiatric Association, 1973-1974; Professor of Psychiatry and Chairman of the Department of Psychiatry, New York

DR. ROBERT R. J. GALLATI
Mt. Vernon, New York
> Deputy Commissioner, Department of Public Safety, Bureau of Police, City of Mt. Vernon, New York; former Director, New York State Identification and Intelligence System; Chairman of the Security and Privacy Committee of Project SEARCH (1969-73) and member of the FBI National Crime Information Center Advisory Policy Board

DOROTHY GLANCY
Washington, D.C.
> Counsel, Subcommittee on Constitutional Rights, U.S. Senate Committee on the Judiciary with responsibility including an investigation of the Special Service Staff's political surveillance unit within the Internal Revenue Service and a four-year survey of personal data banks maintained by federal agencies

HONORABLE BARRY M. GOLDWATER, JR.
Washington, D.C.
> Member of Congress, U.S. House of Representatives; co-author, Omnibus Privacy Bill with U.S. Congressman Edward I. Koch

NAT HENTOFF
New York, New York
> Journalist; co-author of recent book, "State Secrets - Police Surveillance in America"

PROFESSOR SAMUEL B. HOROVITZ
Boston, Massachusetts
  Professor, Suffolk University Law School;
  former Commissioner, National Commission
  on State Workmen's Compensation Laws

CARRIE JOHNSON
Washington, D.C.
  Editorial Writer, *The Washington Post*; former
  legislative Assistant to Honorable Charles McC.
  Mathias, Jr., U.S. Congressman

KENNETH M. KAUFMAN
Washington, D.C.
  Assistant Counsel, Subcommittee on Administrative Practice and Procedure, U.S. Senate
  Committee on the Judiciary, coordinating staff
  investigation on warrantless electronic surveillance

MICHAEL KENNEY
Boston, Massachusetts
  State House Bureau Chief, *The Boston Globe*

MICHAEL S. KEPLINGER
Washington, D.C.
  Attorney, Information Technology Analysis
  Section, National Bureau of Standards, U.S.
  Department of Commerce studying the policy
  impacts of subjects such as privacy and com-
  puter security and proprietary protection for
  computer software

HONORABLE EDWARD I. KOCH
Washington, D.C.
  Member of Congress, U.S. House of Representa-
  tives; co-author, Omnibus Privacy Bill with
  U.S. Congressman Barry M. Goldwater, Jr.

DR. MARGARET LANTIS
Lexington, Kentucky
  Professor of Anthropology, University of Kentucky; Member, Committee on Research Confidentiality, Society for Applied Anthropology

MARY C. LAWTON
Washington, D.C.
  Deputy Assistant Attorney General, Office of
  Legal Counsel, U.S. Department of Justice; has
  participated in the drafting of the Justice
  Department's proposed legislation on the security and privacy of criminal justice information
  systems and in conducting public hearings on
  the Department's proposed regulations covering
  the same subject matter.

DOUGLASS LEA
Washington, D.C.
  Director, Project on Privacy and Data Col-
  lection, American Civil Liberties Union
  Foundation

J. C. R. LICKLIDER
Washington, D.C.
  Director, Information Processing Techniques
  Office, Advanced Research Projects Agency,
  U.S. Department of Defense; presently on leave
  from Project MAC at Massachusetts Institute of
  Technology where his research is principally in
  man-computer communication

JETHRO K. LIEBERMAN
New York, New York
  Attorney; Legal Affairs Editor *Business Week*
  Magazine; author of recent book, "How the
  Government Breaks the Law," among others

F. DRAKE LUNDELL, JR.
Newton, Massachusetts
  Editor, COMPUTERWORLD, national weekly
  newspaper; Editor, Computer Section, *Government Executive* Magazine

PROFESSOR L. THORNE MC CARTY
Buffalo, New York
  Assistant Professor, Faculty of Law and Jurisprudence, State University of New York at
  Buffalo; previously Law and Computer Fellow
  at Stanford Law School and also lecturer in
  law; developed and conducted courses on
  technology and law both at Stanford and State
  University of New York

PROFESSOR GARY T. MARX
Cambridge, Massachusetts
  Associate Professor, Department of Urban
  Studies and Planning (sociology), Massa-
  chusetts Institute of Technology; Senior
  Research Associate, Center for Criminal Justice,
  Harvard Law School; area of interest includes
  civil rights issues — riots, disorder, police,
  black/white race relations in America

HENRI MAZAUD
New York, New York
  Special Assistant, Division of Human Rights,
  United Nations; Doctor of Laws

DOUGLAS METZ
Washington, D.C.
  Deputy Executive Director, President's Domes-
  tic Council Committee on the Right of Privacy;
  Attorney; presently on leave as a vice president
  of the management consultant firm, Booz,
  Allen & Hamilton, Inc.

ALAN OTTEN
Cambridge, Massachusetts
  Fellow, Institute of Politics, John F. Kennedy
  School of Government, Harvard University; on
  leave from *The Wall Street Journal*, where he is
  the Washington Bureau Chief and political
  commentator

JOSEPH OVERTON
Washington, D.C.
  Legislative Assistant to U.S. Congressman
  Barry M. Goldwater, Jr.

VANCE PACKARD
New Canaan, Connecticut
  Author; wrote "The Naked Society" on invasion of privacy in 1964; presently preparing
  another book on this subject

RONALD L. PLESSER
Washington, D.C.
  Attorney associated with Ralph Nader's Center
  for the Study of Responsive Law specializing in
  access to information

HONORABLE CHARLES A. POMEROY
Portland, Maine
  Associate Justice, Maine Supreme Judicial
  Court

PROFESSOR LEOPOLD J. POSPISIL
New Haven, Connecticut
  Professor of Anthropology, Yale University;
  Director, Division of Anthropology, Peabody
  Museum, Yale University

PROFESSOR CHRISTOPHER H. PYLE
New York, New York
  Assistant Professor, City University of New
  York, John Jay College of Criminal Justice;
  Consultant, U.S. Senate Subcommittee on Con-
  stitutional Rights, Committee on the Judiciary;
  publicly disclosed the U.S. Army's surveillance
  of civilian political activity during the 1960's

PROFESSOR HARRY HOWE RANSOM
Nashville, Tennessee
  Chairman, Department of Political Science,
  Vanderbilt University; Specialist in Inter-
  national Politics (American Foreign Policy/
  Decision Making)

CLARK RENNINGER
Washington, D.C.
  Staff Assistant for Computer Utilization Programs, Institute for Computer Sciences and Technology, National Bureau of Standards, U.S. Department of Commerce

HONORABLE CHARLES R. RICHEY
Washington, D.C.
  U.S. District Judge for the District of Columbia

CATHERINE G. RORABACK
Canaan, Connecticut
  Attorney for Griswold before Supreme Court in case of *Griswold vs. Connecticut*

ARNOLD R. ROSENFELD
Boston, Massachusetts
  Attorney; Executive Director, Massachusetts Committee on Criminal Justice; served on the Task Force on Community Crime Prevention of the National Advisory Commission on Criminal Justice Standards and Goals

WILLIAM D. RUCKELSHAUS
Washington, D.C.
  Former U.S. Deputy Attorney General; former Acting Director, Federal Bureau of Investigation

CHARLOTTE SAIKOWSKI
Boston, Massachusetts
  Chief Editorial Writer, *The Christian Science Monitor*; served as diplomatic correspondent in Washington, D.C. for the *Monitor*; covered the USSR for the *Monitor* for five years

PROFESSOR THOMAS M. SCANLON, JR.
Princeton, New Jersey
  Associate Professor of Philosophy, Princeton University; Associate Editor, *Philosophy & Public Affairs*

WALTER L. SCHLENKER
Bridgeport, Connecticut
  Consultant and Chairman, Corporate General Electric Information Standards and Codes Committee; Corporate Information Systems Consulting, General Electric Company

PROFESSOR JUDITH J. THOMSON
Cambridge, Massachusetts
  Professor of Philosophy, Massachusetts Institute of Technology; has published extensively in professional journals

PROFESSOR H. RICHARD UVILLER
New York, New York
  Professor, Columbia University School of Law and Attorney practicing in criminal matters; Former Assistant District Attorney In Charge of Appeals Bureau, New York County; author of forthcoming two-volume casebook on criminal process

PROFESSOR JOSEPH WEIZENBAUM
Cambridge, Massachusetts
  Professor of Computer Science, Massachusetts Institute of Technology; currently on sabbatical at Harvard University as Research Associate in Communications; former Fellow, Center for Advanced Study in the Behavioral Sciences, Stanford, California

CHAIRMAN'S NOTE

William C. Sullivan, former assistant to the director of the FBI (No. 3 man in the FBI), was invited to participate as a Conferee in this Annual Chief Justice Earl Warren Conference that was devoted to the subject of Privacy in a Free Society. Mr. Sullivan served under the directorship of J. Edgar Hoover.

A few weeks prior to the Conference he became ill. Although he could not attend, during his recovery he submitted to us his comments on the background papers prepared for the Conference, along with his personal observations and recommendations on Privacy based on his thirty years' experience in the FBI.

Mr. Sullivan's observations and recommendations are entirely his own and are not the consensus of this Conference.

Mr. Sullivan's paper was not presented to the Conferees at the Conference for discussion in view of his absence.

His comments are presented here in the interest of future study and research.

Theodore I. Koskoff
Conference Chairman

Theodore I. Koskoff, Esq.   June 4, 1974
Chairman, Annual Chief Justice Earl Warren
Conference on Advocacy
20 Garden Street
Cambridge, Massachusetts 02138

Dear Mr. Koskoff:

Since accepting your kind invitation to participate in the Annual Chief Justice Earl Warren Conference, I have had a heart attack. I regret to inform you that I will be unable to come to Cambridge.

As you know from previous correspondence, I have studied the background papers that you sent and was enthusiastically looking forward to discussing them with the authors and the other Conferees. Because I will not be able to do so, however, I have prepared the enclosed thoughts, which include comments on the papers and also my recommendations based on my experience, which I hope will be of value to you.

Again, thank you for the invitation to participate in the Earl Warren Conference. I will always regret my illness prevented me from doing so. The theme of your Conference — Privacy in a Free Society — is one in which I have been deeply interested for years and concerning which I have had some serious doubts but, like a soldier in the midst of battle, have kept them to myself.

You have my every wish for a most successful Conference.

Sincerely yours,

William C. Sullivan
William C. Sullivan

PERSONAL OBSERVATIONS AND RECOMMENDATIONS ON PRIVACY

by William C. Sullivan
Former Assistant to the Director of the FBI

... In framing a government which is to be administered by men over men, the great difficulty lies in this: You must first enable the government to control the governed, and in the next place oblige it *to control itself*.*

The need for the government "to control itself" is certainly most germane to the theme of the Annual Chief Justice Earl Warren Conference, which is devoted this year to "Privacy in a Free Society."

It is remarkably timely when put within the context of the Watergate Affair. The good and just society will not be achieved by the Constitution and our network of laws alone. Both are impotent without men and women who understand them and who have taken a meaningful oath to uphold and to apply the laws equally to all citizens. As we have seen in the recent past there can be no exceptions or the system will break down. At this point the well-known human equation arrives upon the scene. And Gustave Weigel may have been right: "that all human affairs given enough time go badly."

Security operations of the Federal Bureau of Investigation (FBI) have been given time enough to "go badly." What normally would be regarded as Top Secret material has for some time now been appearing regularly in the newspapers. Programs have been abolished and some of those that remain receive widespread publicity. It would be a mistake to think that all of this is harmful. On the contrary this can be quite helpful if it focuses the eyes of the public upon the subject of internal security and as a result of which the entire field is studied exhaustively and systematically for the first time. If this is done properly the people will know for the first time what the security problem really is and what must be done to cope with it successfully.

In the appropriation request of the Federal Bureau of Investigation for 1974 we read:

The FBI's investigative responsibilities in the internal security field cover a broad range of activities which pose clear and present dangers to our society and Government. The work in this field continues to mount and requires a heavy commitment of our resources.

In an earlier appropriation request these responsibilities were set forth in greater detail and mention was made of "espionage, counterespionage, sabotage, treason, sedition, subversion, and related internal security functions" including "Communist Party, USA," its members and sympathizers; communist front groups; totalitarian organizations; as well as other subversive individuals or groups which are alleged to either seek the overthrow of the Government of the United States by force and violence or to conspire against the rights of the citizens."#

---

*The Federalist No. 51 *(my italics)*.

#In this article only one term will be used in its broadest sense to include all the various activities referred to here. This word is "security."

The FBI's authorization to carry out these security responsibilities is based on "legislative enactments, Presidential directives, and instructions of the Attorney General." (Appropriation Hearings for 1972)

I have carefully read the three background papers prepared for the Conference. I have found them to be both thought-provoking and educational. While an estimate of this kind is not easy to make without a discussion in depth with the authors, lacking the benefit of this, I would say that, taking the studies as a whole, I agree with about 75 to 80 percent of what they say.

I will address myself – drawing from my thirty years' experience in the FBI – to privacy (and the lack of it) in a free society: a society, I suggest, which is not nearly as constructively and creatively free as many think or as it ought to and could be. My experiences in the FBI were gathered on different levels including that of Special Agent in the field offices (five in number from east to west), a confidential undercover assignment in Europe during World War II, followed by positions at FBI Headquarters in Washington, D.C. such as Supervisor, Unit Chief, Section Chief, Inspector, Chief Inspector, Assistant Director in Charge of Security and Intelligence Investigations, plus Foreign Operations in Europe, Asia, Latin America and Canada, and lastly, Assistant to the Director in Charge of Investigations in criminal, intelligence, and security which included liaison with our foreign offices.

The following comments I will divide into four sections: (1) Background; (2) Controls; (3) Invasions of Privacy; (4) Final Comments and Recommendations.

Background

Prior to 1939 the FBI was a criminal investigating organization. In 1939 President Franklin D. Roosevelt issued an Executive Order placing the FBI in the field of security and intelligence with major coordinating responsibilities. Literally, this was done overnight.

With the powerful support and encouragement of Franklin D. Roosevelt, the FBI commenced its broad security work and rapidly expanded it as World War II approached to emerge as the coordinator and sole leader in the domestic field. Its origins had become firmly rooted and it was ready for development.

What kind of personnel did we have to work with at that time? We had old veterans of the FBI whose experience was limited to criminal investigations often markedly different from security and intelligence, and young men like myself being hired at a very rapid pace who knew nothing about either criminal or security-intelligence investigations. Who were our instructors? Men equally lacking in authoritative intelligence experience and knowledge. However, much credit should be given to some instructors, who on their own time worked nights, Saturdays and Sundays to learn as much as they could so as to be qualified to instruct effectively.

The leadership of the FBI was opposed to inviting men from the outside to instruct us; men who might know more than we did, at least, about security-intelligence investigations.

The men were aware of this but were powerless to corect the condition.

We were sealed off from the outside world and the experiences and thinking of others from the very beginning, and we remained relatively so and steadily became inbred for thirty years.

In summary, for many years the FBI's main work was the investigation of the violations of the criminal laws over which it had jurisdiction. It was with this work it had established its reputation. Its veterans of years of service thought and taught within the criminal investigating context. Its methods were geared to get results out of criminal investigations. The decisions of the leadership had been mainly limited to this. The entire FBI had been structured for and remained structured essentially around the methodology of criminal investigations. Yet, now it was expected at once to do both. Could it handle both efficiently without being *basically reorganized*? It tried. It is still trying.

It was with this background that special agents were sent forth from the Bureau's Headquarters to handle one of the most complex, difficult, important and controversial responsibilities of our government – the conducting of security and intelligence operations, which had for their major objective the making of a substantial contribution to our overall national security interests.

However, there was a positive and productive side also. It was to be found in the innate ability, industry, common sense and good will of the great majority of special agents. Without proper leadership, training and guidance they did, in those early days, a reasonably good job. But FBI Headquarters was wrong in releasing to the American people propaganda that pictured us as an elite corps far superior to any other governmental organization, federal, state or local. The gulf between public relations and our actual performances were indeed very great. Not many on the outside knew of this gulf. You might say the FBI concealed it by "classifying" it. As indicated, our actual performances were reasonably good and I think the public would agree, but it is on this factual basis we should have remained and not on some unreal level in the realms of fiction. The strength of the FBI has always been the good men in the field offices, the special agents who like the work and who give their lives to the Bureau "unknown and unsung." The weaknesses of the FBI have always been the leadership in Washington, of which I was a part for fifteen years; I accept my share of blame for its serious shortcomings.

May I suggest that the men who spent the best years of their lives in the FBI do not want to be spared any criticism or any public exposure of their shortcomings. This is a first step toward any effective remedial measure. At the same time it is believed that if our constructive critics personally experienced what the men of the FBI experienced year in and year out and what they had to do to get positive results, our critics would not wonder so much as to why more was not accomplished, but rather they would wonder how the men of the FBI accomplished as much as they did under conditions which then were never conducive to change, experimentation and progress.

It is important to realize that the agents began in the field offices in a pre-war atmosphere to be followed soon by World War II, in which we were all convinced we were fighting for the survival of our nation. The enemy was real. In this nation, with sabotage attempts and other problems facing it, the overall enemy consisted of Bundists and native fascists in support of the Axis powers, and their espionage agents. To be candid, the "right to privacy" was not at issue nor was it an impediment to solving cases. It mattered not whether electronic devices or other techniques were used. The issues were black and white and crystal clear. The methodology was pragmatic: will it work; will it get the necessary results? The primacy of civil liberties on occasions gave way to expediency. President Franklin D. Roosevelt posed no barrier to this method and, for me, this was no criticism of him at that perilous time.

Such a very great man as Franklin D. Roosevelt saw nothing wrong in asking the FBI to investigate those opposing his lend-lease policy – a purely political request. He also had us look into the activities of others who opposed our entrance into World War II just as later administrations had the FBI look into those opposing the conflict in Vietnam. It was a political request also when he instructed us to put a telephone tap, a microphone and a physical surveillance on an internationally-known leader in his Administration. It was done; the results he wanted secured and given to him. Certain records of this kind and others were not then or later put into the regular filing system. Rather, they were deliberately kept out of it. Electronic devices were used freely all through World War II, with a minimum of controls. President Roosevelt made requests of various kinds.

The FBI security operations developed through a pre-war psychology which was quickly transformed into a war psychology. In a very real sense it has breathed, lived and worked within the framework of this war psychology ever since. World War II was followed by the Korean War which in turn was followed by the Vietnam conflict. Permeating our entire nation on the home front was the Cold War. Hence, just as a soldier on the field of battle did not consider it wrong to kill the enemy, so, too, on the home front it was not considered wrong in major cases to use extraordinary measures in security work. The same enemy was before both. Both had the same goal — vanquish the enemy. We did not consider this unlawful.*

The objectives and methodology were the same under all administrations to a greater or lesser degree, Republican and Democratic alike.

Controls

As I said previously, there was relatively little control over the use of electronic devices in the 40's and the invasion of privacy was not a major concern — unless one got caught. Gradually, during the fifties more and more controls were developed and I must say, that fewer electronic devices were ultimately used than is generally accepted by those who oppose their use. For example, when I left the FBI in 1971 we had, in a country of over 200 million people with much lawlessness going on, only a few microphones in use. This number had been reduced steadily over a period of time. Telephone surveillances were much more numerous but even these were not as great as many thought. (I refer now only to the FBI where my knowledge on the subject ends.) But the word was out based on previously widespread use of electronic devices. Suspicion was rampant, and how can you easily eliminate such belief and the concerns and fears which flow from it.

Invasion of Privacy

The use of electronic listening devices do constitute an invasion of privacy. Of course, much of this has been rationalized down through the years. A person holding the contrary view is either totally ignorant of the subject matter or is deliberately not telling the truth. And, who can deny that such an invasion of privacy is in violation of our Bill of Rights. Why is it done then? I would add to pragmatism the old principle: "the end justifies the means." Herein lies the real danger of electronic devices to any society struggling to retain its freedom. Yet, this principle is widely used in all major segments of American society.

To repeat, why then is this done, and by established government agencies? Could it be that the Annual Chief Justice Earl Warren Conference might find an interesting and fertile clue (but not the complete answer) in the studies conducted by Dr. Stanley Milgram at Yale University and published under the title of *Obedience and Authority*. Dr. Milgram adapted from his book an article captioned "The Perils of Obedience," published in *Harper's Magazine*, December 1973.

Dr. Milgram writes:
> The extreme willingness of adults to go to almost any lengths on the command of authority constitutes the chief findings of the study and the fact most urgently demanding an explanation.

Dr. Milgram concludes:
> This is, perhaps, the most fundamental lesson of our study; ordinary people simply doing their jobs, and without any particular hostility on their part, can become agents in a terrible destructive process. Moreover, even when the destructive efforts of their work become patently clear, and they are asked to carry out actions incompatible with fundamental standards of morality, relatively few people have the resources needed to resist authority. ... The essence of obedience is that a person comes to view himself as an instrument for

---

*Bear in mind that what we did in the FBI emanated from courses of instruction in government schools and conferences, and was regarded as government policy officially sanctioned down through the years and issued under orders.

carrying out another person's wishes, and he therefore no longer regards himself as responsible for his actions. . . . Thus there is a fragmentation of the total human act; no one is confronted with the consequences of his decision to carry out the evil act. The person who assumes responsibility has evaporated. Perhaps this is the most common characteristic of socially organized evil in modern society.

If this is true only in part, what bearing would you say it has had during the past thirty years (as we all know some techniques go back far beyond this) on the use of telephone surveillances, microphones, cameras, informants,* special sources, classified dossiers and other related techniques? What can be done about it, keeping in mind the human equation; the many unique and varied *foibles of human nature*? How can we unsnarl it and make our laws adhered to despite the intermingling of our different degrees of freedom and limitation? The same basic question applies to *corruption* in law enforcement which has always existed and gets worse as we get larger and larger and more complex as a society. While none of us will agree in full with Voltaire, there is a grain of disturbing truth in his observation: "a collection of crimes, follies, and misfortunes" in the history of mankind.

Final Comments and Recommendations

I have mentioned that I agree with about 75-80 percent of the reasoning and information set forth in the Conference papers. My disagreements which, because of time and space I will not submit in full, relate to such matters as these:

I. Value of electronic devices. Although I agree with positions taken by former Attorney General Ramsey Clark, I do not agree with his statement appearing in the Conference background paper on electronic surveillance where he tends to minimize the importance of tapping to our national security. The value of electronic devices has been seriously underestimated in some instances, especially in the counterespionage field. I know of many instances – in both the intelligence and criminal areas – where electronic surveillance has proven to be effective.

I want to be clear on this point. I am not saying the value of the devices justifies the invasion of privacy. That is another issue. I am saying the value of electronic devices is greater than some realize. Additionally, there are electronic devices now going beyond the limitations of the old fashioned telephone surveillance and microphone which should be taken into consideration.

II. Statistics are always difficult to vouch for without reservations. Statistics in the field of law enforcement and intelligence have for years and years left much to be desired, if I may make an understatement. This is a field which should be studied exhaustively, modernized and factualized from "the ground up." If accurate statistics are not developed and given to scholars then what good are they? Years ago in business (and perhaps today in some cases) *two sets of books* were kept, the one for public inspections and the real one not for public inspection. Perhaps in some cases we have this problem with statistics.

III. Reference has been made in the papers to surveillance of "political activities." We can agree at once that intelligence and law enforcement generally have not been fully separated from politics. On the other hand, it is most important to make the correct distinctions between "political surveillances," and, I will add, *investigations* and legitimate security or intelligence surveillances and investigations. It is not a black and white matter. The gray areas are everywhere present requiring careful thought, objective analysis and

---

*In the FBI the *informant* assumed the work of what is described in at least one of the Conference papers as work of an informer. The FBI had no need for this distinction.

prudent action. The dividing line may be an overt or covert act which is in violation of the law. It would seem to me *better definitions* are needed here.

Recommendations

I. A federal government Commission be established, staffed with qualified scholars, to make an exhaustive examination to determine in this nation the following:

   A. What is internal or domestic security (viewed as a part of, but not the same as, national security which extends beyond our boundary lines as a nation and deals with additional and different subject matters)?

      1. Does internal or domestic security actually need a security and intelligence system to protect this nation (I refer to federal)?

         a. If not, give full, factual justification.

            (1) Could the states handle whatever is needed in this field?

         b. If needed, give a full, factual justification.

            (1) What should be its scope, its limitations, objectives, methodology (i.e., techniques, devices, programs and guidelines?

II. If it is decided that an internal security and intelligence system is necessary, that it be removed from the FBI and established under an independent *Board* selected by Congress and representative of the main segments of the population of the country: Labor, Science, Education, Business, Press, Government, Intellectual, Religion, and Law Enforcement. It should be selected, of course, without any regard for race, color, creed, sex and wholly nonpartisan. The Board would appoint the Director whose term should be limited to five years and each Board member limited to a three-year term with a new one to be selected each year (change is a healthy thing). The Board would consist of nine members.

   A. Advantages

      1. The FBI as it is now structured is a potential threat to our civil liberties; recent events indicate this. It has become a vast, powerful organization of over 20,000 members with a budget for the 1974 fiscal year of $366,506,000, a net increase of $14,831,000, 4.2 percent above the $351,675,000 appropriated for the 1973 fiscal year. This budget could actually be reduced substantially. To separate the security and intelligence operations from the FBI would reduce significantly the *power* of the FBI.

      2. It would help greatly in removing the FBI from politics and politics from the FBI. (This would be a tremendous accomplishment for the good of our country.)

      3. Mention has been made of having the Oversight Committee of Congress take charge of and control security and intelligence operations. In the light of what I have witnessed during the past thirty years, I would be unalterably opposed. It could make such operations just as politically enmeshed as before if *not more so*. Such operations should be wholly independent of the White House, the Department of Justice and all other Departments and have a *buffer in the form of the Board* just described existing between it and Congress. *There should be no unilateral or direct liaison or relations between an independent domestic security and intelligence system or agency and the White House and Congress.* All liaison and requests from these places and others should be funneled through the Board. A request could be made of one person in confidence that never would be made of a Board of many members. The Board should make the decision if the request is proper and action should be taken. If so, instructions to meet the request would be given by the

Board to the Director of "Security and Intelligence."*

4. It would result in far greater efficiency. Criminal investigators do not usually make good security and intelligence agents and vice versa.

III. Informants. An informant is a spy to some degree or other and for different periods of time. These people need to be selected for quality, access to needed information and should be tightly controlled. If you take live informants out of criminal and security-intelligence operations, there can be no doubt about the reduction of efficiency and positive results. I admit the development and use of informants is a distasteful function. So is arresting or shooting a man for a law violation.

As to the value of an informant or a spy, I suggest that you read the most interesting and enlightening book entitled "The Shattered Silence" (the Eli Cohen Affair) by Zwy Aldouby and Jerrold Ballinger. The facts in this book speak for themselves.

IV. Consideration should be given to have the government issue an order that no telephone surveillances or microphones be used by any federal agency during the next three years. At the very same time a vehicle should be set up to study for that three-year period the effects of this ban to determine if the criminal and security-intelligence investigations suffered from the ban or not. The study should be done by knowledgeable men not employed by an investigative agency but authorized to have access to all the necessary evidence.

V. Classification. This system is still in real need of being fundamentally revised. For too long too much material has been classified along with "classifying" mistakes, failures, irregularities, illegalities and other activities. This is one reason for the alienation between youth and government; between adults, also, and officials of our government.

VI. I recommend strongly that a truly objective, serious Commission be established to make the most exhaustive study possible of internal security and security-intelligence organizations and investigations and come up with some clear, incisive answers and recommendations in order to strike a balance between the need for national security and the preservation of civil liberties, among them the right to privacy.

I urge my fellow citizens to give some serious thought to these recommendations based on thirty years' experience.

The FBI of the future should not be the creation of any one man or any special groups within government. The FBI of the future should be the creation of the best and most informed minds we have in the country, both inside and outside of government. One way to get a movement started in this direction is through public conferences.

The Annual Chief Justice Earl Warren Conference on Advocacy of June 6 and 7, 1974, is a creative step in the right direction. It will deal with an extremely important subject directly related to the work of the FBI: "Privacy in a Free Society." I am sure we will all agree though, that this is only one of many important phases which go to make up the total responsibilities and work of the FBI. In view of this, may I urge that interested men and women who attend this Conference give continuing thought to arranging, as soon as possible, a series of conferences, numerous enough to give exhaustive study to all major segments of the work of the FBI. Members of the FBI and others in related areas should, of course, be invited and, in fact, such a series of conferences would suffer seriously from their absence. From these meetings should follow a set of specific and detailed recommendations for completely reorganizing and renewing the FBI, which will be in keeping not alone with our traditional values but also with a profoundly changing social order on the threshold of a new era.

---

*This does not mean that Congress should not be in control. It should be but it must be Congress and not individual politicians. A Board such as I outlined could guarantee this much-to-be-desired result.

LIFETIME FELLOWS OF THE FOUNDATION

The Lifetime Fellows of the Roscoe Pound-American Trial Lawyers Foundation are recognized for their continuous support of research endeavors in the intensive pursuit of truth for the ultimate goal of more effective administration of justice for all.

James S. Abatiell
Rutland, Vermont

James H. Ackerman
Long Beach, California

Thomas T. Anderson
Indio, California

Ashcraft & Gerel
Washington, D.C.

William I. Aynes
Atlanta, Georgia

Russell M. Baker
Dallas, Texas

Honorable Joseph G. Barbieri
Elizabeth, New Jersey

A. William Barlow
Honolulu, Hawaii

Chester Bedell
Jacksonville, Florida

Nathan Bedell
Jacksonville, Florida

Herbert H. Bennett
Portland, Maine

Ralph R. Benson
Hollywood, California

Charles F. Blanchard
Raleigh, North Carolina

Milton M. Blumenthal
Chicago, Illinois

George A. Boyle
Bakersfield, California

Ellis B. Brannon
Cleveland, Ohio

Louis T. Brindisi
Utica, New York

Walter W. Brooks
Columbia, South Carolina

John A. Burgess
Montpelier, Vermont

Evan H. Callanan
Westland, Michigan

Richard J. Cardali
New York, New York

LIFETIME FELLOWS OF THE FOUNDATION

Thomas E. Cargill, Jr.
Boston, Massachusetts

Jessie B. Carnevale
Las Vegas, Nevada

Rex Carr
East St. Louis, Illinois

Robert E. Cartwright
San Francisco, California

Clinton W. Chapman
Washington, D.C.

Samuel Charfoos
Southfield, Michigan

Stanley M. Chesley
Cincinnati, Ohio

Neil H. Chonin
Miami, Florida

Edward H. Cloutier
Livermore Falls, Maine

Arthur Cobb
Baton Rouge, Louisiana

Al J. Cone
West Palm Beach, Florida

Bobby Lee Cook
Summerville, Georgia

James E. Coonley, II
Hampton, Iowa

John F. Corcoran
Tucson, Arizona

Roy Daubenspeck
Plaistow, New Hampshire

Peter A. Davis
Ann Arbor, Michigan

Robert R. Disbro
Cleveland, Ohio

John E. Dolan, Jr.
Patchogue, New York

Joseph C. Dwyer
Olean, New York

J. Robert Dyment
San Diego, California

Irving M. Einbinder
Hagerstown, Maryland

Arnold B. Elkind
New York, New York

J. Newton Esdaile
Boston, Massachusetts

Donald J. Farage
Philadelphia, Pennsylvania

Moody M. Farhart
Minot, North Dakota

Millard C. Farmer, Jr.
Newnan, Georgia

Albert S. Fein
Philadelphia, Pennsylvania

Stanley L. Feldstein
Old San Juan, Puerto Rico

Ray Ferrero, Jr.
Fort Lauderdale, Florida

Philip R. Finkelmeier
Cincinnati, Ohio

Richard S. Fleisher
Chicago, Illinois

Daniel Fogel
Los Angeles, California

Abraham E. Freedman
Philadelphia, Pennsylvania

Philip S. Frey
Honolulu, Hawaii

Lawrence B. Friedman
North Miami Beach, Florida

Jacob D. Fuchsberg
New York, New York

E. S. Gallon
Dayton, Ohio

Harold M. Gamer
Beverly Hills, California

John Gardenal
San Francisco, California

Gustavo A. Gelpi
Old San Juan, Puerto Rico

LIFETIME FELLOWS OF THE FOUNDATION

John Phillips Godfrey
Many, Louisiana

John Michael Goldberg
Chicago, Illinois

Burl L. Green
Portland, Oregon

Herbert E. Greestone
Newark, New Jersey

Herbert Hafif
Claremont, California

Oliver Wendell Hasenflue
Avon Lake, Ohio

William W. Hawkins
Kingsport, Tennessee

Thomas L. Hennessey
Towson, Maryland

Russ M. Herman
New Orleans, Louisiana

Lawrence P. Hickey
Chicago, Illinois

Arthur C. Hodgson
Lyons, Kansas

Frank D. Holcomb
Marietta, Georgia

John F. Holcomb
Hamilton, Ohio

Herbert B. Hulse
Goldsboro, North Carolina

John K. Hyun
Honolulu, Hawaii

Frank C. Ingraham
Nashville, Tennessee

Hesper A. Jackson, Jr.
Brooklyn, New York

Morris I. Jaffee
Dallas, Texas

Frank Joseph Janik, Jr.
Amherst, Ohio

Joseph L. Jerger
Mansfield, Ohio

William E. Johnson
Frankfort, Kentucky

E. Stewart Jones, Jr.
Troy, New York

Tom G. Jones
Franklin, Indiana

Leo S. Karlin
Chicago, Illinois

Joseph Kelner
New York, New York

John J. Kennelly
Chicago, Illinois

Frederick S. Klein
Tucson, Arizona

Sidney B. Klovsky
Philadelphia, Pennsylvania

Elmo E. Koos, Sr.
Peoria, Illinois

Theodore I. Koskoff
Bridgeport, Connecticut

Myron W. Kronisch
Newark, New Jersey

David H. Kubert
Philadelphia, Pennsylvania

Norman J. Landau
New York, New York

Samuel Langerman
Phoenix, Arizona

J. D. Lee
Madisonville, Tennessee

Max M. Librach
St. Louis, Missouri

George Alexander McKray
San Francisco, California

V. Eugene McMichen
Austell, Georgia

Joseph D. Maher, Jr.
Newark, New Jersey

William Aden Mann
Chevy Chase, Maryland

LIFETIME FELLOWS OF THE FOUNDATION

Richard M. Markus
Cleveland, Ohio

Joe L. Maynes
Aberdeen, South Dakota

Leonard B. Melvin, Jr.
Laurel, Mississippi

Esau J. Mishkin
Mineola, New York

Daniel R. Monaco
Naples, Florida

Thomas Owen Morgan
Rockville Centre, New York

Martin J. Murphy
Colorado Springs, Colorado

Harvey B. Nachman
Old San Juan, Puerto Rico

John E. Norton
Belleville, Illinois

Melvin O. Nuss
Great Bend, Kansas

Cornelius C. O'Brien, Jr.
Philadelphia, Pennsylvania

James P. O'Flarity
Fort Lauderdale, Florida

Dr. Jack H. Olender
Washington, D.C.

Nat P. Ozmon
Chicago, Illinois

Roger L. Pardieck
Seymour, Indiana

Parker, Battaglia, Parker,
Ross and Stolba
St. Petersburg, Florida

Paty, Lawrence & Lawrence
Chattanooga, Tennessee

R. W. Payne, Jr.
Miami, Florida

Rudolph T. Pelletier
Madawaska, Maine

Stephen Andrew Perel
Houston, Texas

Harry M. Pippin
Williston, North Dakota

Paul L. Pratt
East Alton, Illinois

J. Ward Rafferty
New London, Connecticut

Louis J. Richman, Jr.
Newport News, Virginia

Dean A. Robb
Traverse City, Michigan

Saul I. Ruman
Hammond, Indiana

John W. Russell
Carlinville, Illinois

Stanley E. Sacks
Norfolk, Virginia

E. B. Sahlstrom
Eugene, Oregon

John Burley Scales
Boonville, Indiana

David Schack
New York, New York

Perry J. Shertz
Wilkes-Barre, Pennsylvania

George E. Shibley
Long Beach, California

Samuel Shore
Los Angeles, California

Sindell, Sindell, Bourne,
Stern & Spero
Cleveland, Ohio

Abner R. Sisson
Boston, Massachusetts

Cawood Smith
Harlan, Kentucky

Charles W. Smith
Saco, Maine

Lester Berry Smith, Jr.
Peoria, Illinois

Richard N. Solman
Caribou, Maine

LIFETIME FELLOWS OF THE FOUNDATION

Craig Spangenberg
Cleveland, Ohio

Robert K. Steinberg
Beverly Hills, California

Stewart & DeChant
Company, L.P.A.
Cleveland, Ohio

Robert C. Strodel
Peoria, Illinois

William Lawrence Summers
Cleveland, Ohio

Glenn J. Tabor
Valparaiso, Indiana

Daniel B. Tallon
Glens Falls, New York

John B. Tittmann
Albuquerque, New Mexico

Jack A. Travis
Jackson, Mississippi

Traxler, Malkoff & Boyd
Company, L.P.A.
Youngstown, Ohio

Edward E. Triviz
Las Cruces, New Mexico

Meyer M. Ueoka
Wailuku, Hawaii

Lewis V. Vafiades
Bangor, Maine

Bill Wagner
Tampa, Florida

Solomon Wasserman
Minneapolis, Minnesota

George F. West, Jr.
Natchez, Mississippi

Louis Wiener, Jr.
Las Vegas, Nevada

David E. Williams
Richland, Washington

Williams, Trine and Greenstein
Boulder, Colorado

Robert B. Willson
Asheville, North Carolina

Leon Wolfstone
Seattle, Washington